BTEC Level 2 First Study Skills Guide in Land and Environment

Welcome to your Study Skills Guide! You can make it your own – start by adding your personal and course details below...

Learner's name: _____

BTEC course title: _____

Date started: _____

Mandatory units:

_____

_____

_____

Optional units:

_____

_____

_____

Centre name: _____

Centre address:

_____

_____

Tutor's name: _____

Published by Pearson Education Limited, a company incorporated in England and Wales, having its registered office at Edinburgh Gate, Harlow, Essex, CM20 2JE. Registered company number: 872828

Edexcel is a registered trademark of Edexcel Limited

Text © Pearson Education Limited 2010

First published 2010

2020
17

British Library Cataloguing in Publication Data
A catalogue record for this book is available from the British Library

ISBN 978 1 84690 925 2

Typeset and edited by DSM Partnership
Cover design by Visual Philosophy, created by eMC Design
Cover photo © Visual Photos/Tanya Constantine
Printed in Great Britain by Ashford Colour Press Ltd., Gosport, Hampshire

Acknowledgements
The publisher would like to thank the following for their kind permission to reproduce their photographs (Key: b-bottom; c-centre; l-left; r-right; t-top):

Alamy Images: ACE STOCK LIMITED 55; Corbis: 5, 60; iStockphoto: Ryan Alexander 72cl, Joachim Angeltun 78br, ryan burke 75t, Steven Foley 76b, Julien Grondin 70l, Alex van de Hoef 71bl, 77cl, Alex van de Hoef 71bl, 77cl, Diane Labombarbe 78bl, David H. Lewis 40, Iolon 71cl, Alex Mathers 77tc, joaquin perales 72cr, pialhovik 70r, Leah Sisson 37, Mark Stay 78t, Stephen Sweet 76t, Willie B. Thomas 11, wdstock 48, John Woodcock 72tr, 77cr; Pearson Education Ltd: Steve Shott 24, Ian Wedgewood 35; Photolibrary.com: Eline de Ruiter 71cr; Shutterstock: 71br, 75b, 78c, Barry Barnes 72tl, Stephen Finn 72tc, Vallentin Vassileff 73; TopFoto: John Powell 20. All other images © Pearson Education

Every effort has been made to trace the copyright holders and we apologise in advance for any unintentional omissions. We would be pleased to insert the appropriate acknowledgement in any subsequent edition of this publication.

Websites
Go to www.pearsonhotlinks.co.uk to gain access to the relevant website links and information on how they can aid your studies. When you access the site, search for either the title BTEC Level 2 First in Land and Environment or the ISBN 9781846909252.

Disclaimer
This material has been published on behalf of Edexcel and offers high-quality support for the delivery of Edexcel qualifications. This does not mean that the material is essential to achieve any Edexcel qualification, nor does it mean that it is the only suitable material available to support any Edexcel qualification. Edexcel material will not be used verbatim in setting any Edexcel examination or assessment. Any resource lists produced by Edexcel shall include this and other appropriate resources.Copies of official specifications for all Edexcel qualifications may be found on the Edexcel website: www.edexcel.com

Contents

Popular progression pathways

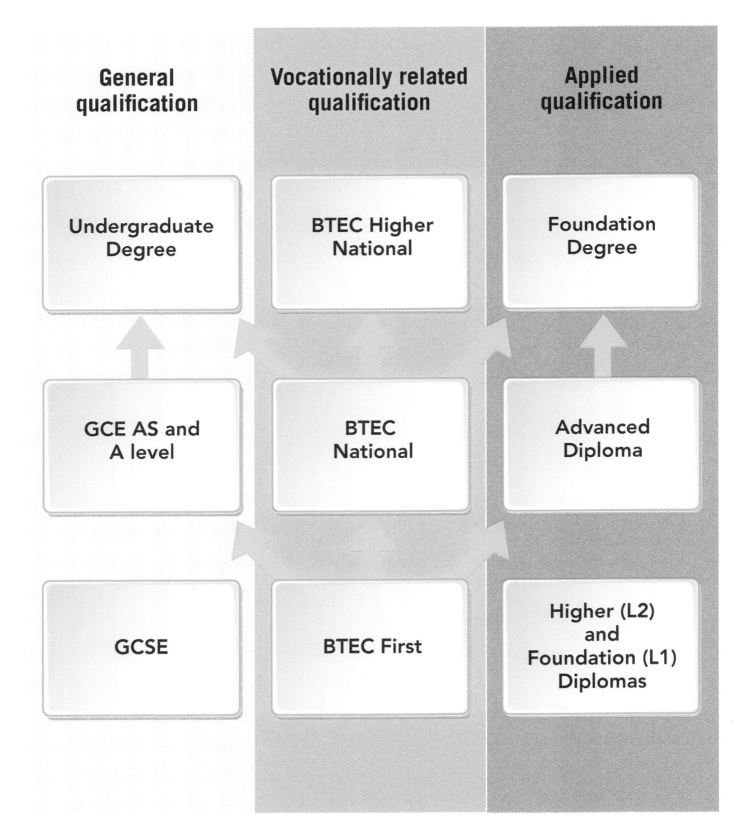

General qualification

Undergraduate Degree

GCE AS and A level

GCSE

Vocationally related qualification

BTEC Higher National

BTEC National

BTEC First

Applied qualification

Foundation Degree

Advanced Diploma

Higher (L2) and Foundation (L1) Diplomas

Your BTEC First course
Early days

Every year many new learners start BTEC Level 2 First courses, enjoy the challenge and successfully achieve their award. Some do this the easy way; others make it harder for themselves.

Everyone will have different feelings when they start their course.

Case study: Sara prepares to begin her BTEC First in Animal Husbandry

The letter arrived during the summer holidays to let me know I'd been accepted at college to study animal husbandry. This was going to be one of the biggest steps I'd ever taken. I'd not been in a classroom with others for a long time as I'd been schooled at home for the last five years.

This was my time to choose what I wanted for a future career and I was determined that it was going to involve being outside. My tutor was really kind to me when we met, and she suggested that I used the determined feelings that I had to combat some of the fears I was feeling about coming to college. She also told me that meeting new people would build my confidence and that everyone would be feeling slightly anxious on their first day.

My tutor wasn't wrong. It turned out that nobody knew each other, and we all looked pretty scared on that first day. Looking back now, it was totally normal to feel that way. Our tutor asked everyone to write three words to describe how we each felt, and she joined in too. I was surprised that everyone in the room wrote 'nervous', even my tutor! This made me feel much better and I started to feel really excited about the coming year.

- Write down three words that describe how you are feeling as you start your course.

About your course

What do you know already?

If someone asks you about your course, could you give a short, accurate description? If you can, you have a good understanding of what your course is about. This has several benefits.

Four benefits of understanding your course

1. You will be better prepared and organised.

2. You can make links between the course and the world around you.

3. You can check how your personal interests and hobbies relate to the course.

4. You will be alert to information that relates to topics you are studying, whether it's from conversations with family and friends, watching television or at a part-time job.

Read any information you have been given by your centre. Also check the Edexcel website for further details – go to www.edexcel.com.

Interest/hobby	How this relates to my studies

What else do you need to know?

Five facts you should find out about your course

1   The type of BTEC qualification you are studying.

2   How many credits your qualification is worth.

3   The number of mandatory units you will study and what they cover.

4   How many credits the mandatory units are worth.

5   The number of optional units you need to study in total and the options available in your centre.

Case study: From farm to classroom

Simon is getting ready to start his BTEC First in Agriculture at college. He is very happy that he only has to attend college for four days a week as this means he can continue to work on the family farm.

Simon has worked with his family on the farm since he was old enough to walk and he doesn't really see the need for college. He thinks he has all the skills and knowledge he needs to run a successful farm as he has watched his father do it for many years. It is Simon's father who has encouraged his son to study further. He is keen for his son to bring fresh ideas to the farm once he has completed his studies.

Although he has many practical skills in arable farming, Simon has little background knowledge on why things are done the way they are. When he looks through the course structure with his father, he soon realises that there will be many new skills to be learnt, and sessions on farm machinery, estate maintenance and livestock farming have especially captured his interest.

Simon is quite worried about the time that will be spent inside a classroom as he doesn't feel he is very academic. His tutor has reassured him that the theory taught in the classroom will always cover subjects in which he has a keen interest. He also finds out he will be completing functional skills in ICT, which means he'll be able to show his father a thing or two about keeping farm records on a computer instead of in a pile on the kitchen table!

• What are you looking forward to doing most on your course?

BTEC FACT

BTEC First Certificate = 15 credits

BTEC First Extended Certificate = 30 credits

BTEC First Diploma = 60 credits

Generally, the more credits there are, the longer it takes to study for the qualification.

TRY THIS

Find out which optional units your centre offers. To check the topics covered in each unit go to www.edexcel.com.

TOP TIPS

If you have a choice of optional units in your centre and are struggling to decide, talk through your ideas with your tutor.

Activity: How well do you know your course?

Complete this activity to check that you know the main facts. Compare your answers with a friend. You should have similar answers except where you make personal choices, such as about optional units. Your tutor can help you complete task 9.

1 The correct title of the BTEC award I am studying is:

2 The length of time it will take me to complete my award is:

3 The number of mandatory units I have to study is:

4 The titles of my mandatory units, and their credit values, are:

5 The main topics I will learn in each mandatory unit include:

Mandatory unit	Main topics

6 The number of credits I need to achieve by studying optional units is:

7 The titles of my optional units, and their credit values, are:

8 The main topics I will learn in each optional unit include:

Optional unit	Main topics

9 Other important aspects of my course are:

10 After I have achieved my BTEC First, my options include:

Introduction to the BTEC Firsts in land and environment subjects

Welcome to the exciting and diverse world of land and environment. Whether you choose to study agriculture, animal care, countryside and environment, fish husbandry, floristry, horse care, horticulture or land-based technology, you will develop the skills and qualities needed to follow your chosen career path on this course.

During your course you will have the chance to investigate many different and exciting careers within your chosen sector and you'll receive helpful advice from your tutors throughout. You may also be introduced to career paths you didn't even realise existed, so keep your mind open to the options available to you.

Your course may cover horse care or something completely different.

An enthusiastic work ethic is an essential skill to develop for all land and environment jobs. The work is hard and these are not your average 9 to 5 careers, although having said that, working in the land and environment industries is extremely rewarding. Employers will be looking for new staff with the skills needed in the industry and the confidence to bring new and exciting ideas to their companies.

At this early stage of your course, make a list of some of the things you already know about the area you are studying. Don't worry if you can't think of very much to write now, it will be useful to look back at this when you reach the end of your course to see what you have learnt.

Throughout this course, you will be introduced to many career opportunities and you may also take part in work experience. What types of jobs appeal to you within your chosen land and environment sector?

Case study: Sam's garden business

Sam completed a BTEC First Diploma in Horticulture in 2005 and now runs a very successful landscaping business.

"When I started college, my mind was set on becoming a garden centre manager. At that time, I worked in a garden centre and wanted to work my way up in the company. But during college my career started heading in a different direction.

"During the BTEC First, my interest in landscaping started to develop. I began to learn why certain plants grew well together. I designed and planted seasonal bedding schemes, and I helped to lay pathways and erect fencing with National Diploma learners. I even won an award at college for my individual garden project.

I completed my work experience with a local landscape design company, which offered me a job when I completed my course.

"However, after successfully completing my First Diploma I decided to study for a National Diploma in Horticulture rather than take the job offered to me. I gained a huge amount of knowledge and many practical skills during my time at college which has enabled me to start up my own landscaping company.

"After six months in business, I was able to purchase my own truck to carry my tools. I now have two vehicles, a large amount of tools and machinery and work that I have to turn away. Going to college was the best thing I ever did, and I've never looked back."

Skills you need for land and environment

Working safely

Whether you are working with animals, plants and flowers, with machinery, tools and equipment, or with other people, keeping yourself and others around you safe at all times is essential. It should be at the forefront of everything you do.

Being flexible

Working in the land and environment industries needs a flexible attitude. There could be times when you will need to turn your hand to other tasks that are not necessarily within your remit. Being flexible with time is an important skill as the weather can have a huge impact on what you do, and when you do it. Working during cool parts of the day may mean early starts during the summer months and birthing animals may mean very late nights.

Organisation

Being organised is an essential skill and is needed for things to go smoothly. Many land and environment industries experience extra demand at key dates during the year, such as Christmas, Valentine's Day, Mother's Day, Easter and Halloween, as well as having tight seasonal schedules. An organised staff will allow a business to satisfy demand before these key dates and to meet its schedules, and to stay successful for years to come.

Dealing with the public

Some areas of the land and environment sector will involve dealing with members of the public. This will be the case if you work in:

- garden centres or nurseries
- floristry
- landscape gardening
- rescue centres
- zoos and wildlife parks
- petting farms
- team building centres
- horse riding instruction
- park ranging
- shoot organising
- teaching or training.

Other jobs may involve dealing with companies as your customers. These could be:

- small village shops
- large supermarket chains
- estate properties
- parks and gardens
- hotel chains
- local councils
- overseas companies
- vets
- event organisers.

Keeping customers happy is an important skill that you will develop over time and with experience. Several other skills may be needed when dealing with people. Some of these skills are listed below.

Verbal and non-verbal communication skills

Your tone of voice and non-verbal actions may have more impact on a customer or colleague than what you actually say. You should learn to:

- make good eye contact
- use the correct tone of voice
- hold a good posture
- know the difference between formal and informal communication.

Written communication skills

Written communication includes letters, emails, memos, texts, reports, and material on notice boards and displays. Accuracy is vital in all written communication. If your written work is full of mistakes, it creates a bad impression; if it also contains inaccurate information, problems could occur.

Telephone skills

Good telephone technique ensures repeat business. Mobile technology allows many organisations to conduct much of their business by mobile phone or over the internet – even when in the middle of a field, stable or woodland. Be aware that even if you are in the middle of a stressful job, you should come across as a professional. If it is really inconvenient to speak, explain this to your caller politely. Ask when it would be convenient to call back, and remember to call back at the requested time.

Negotiation skills

Negotiating prices when both selling and buying goods is essential for any successful land and environment business. If you do not feel confident with this aspect of your job, make sure you ask someone more senior to go through the stages of a negotiation with you. You can practise on your friends when you want something from them, or when you want them to do something that they initially don't want to do.

IT skills

Being 'computer literate' has become a standard requirement for many jobs and being able to use technology is a necessary skill. Information and communication technologies are now used by the majority of land and environment organisations for many tasks, such as finding information, producing reports, generating invoices, storing data and banking.

Foreign language skills

The land and environment sector in the UK employs many foreign nationals and while their English is usually very good, you may find it useful to have some expertise in other languages. It will be especially important to develop your listening skills.

Teamwork

Being able to work effectively as part of a team is a skill that is expected by many employers. Many land and environment jobs involve hard work, and having a team to support you is crucial as it enables you to work more efficiently. Being part of a team usually means that you forge strong working relationships with those around you.

Teamwork is one area of the personal, learning and thinking skills that you will develop as you are undertaking your BTEC programme.

Before you start your course, list what you think are your strongest skills.

More about BTEC Level 2 Firsts

What is different about a BTEC Level 2 First?

How you learn

Expect to be 'hands-on'. BTEC Level 2 Firsts are practical and focus on the skills and knowledge needed in the workplace. You will learn new things and learn how to apply your knowledge.

BTEC First learners are expected to take responsibility for their own learning and be keen and well-organised. You should enjoy having more freedom, while knowing you can still ask for help or support if you need it.

How you are assessed

Many BTEC First courses are completed in one year, but if you are taking GCSEs as well, you may be doing it over two years or more. You will be assessed by completing **assignments** written by your tutors. These are based on **learning outcomes** set by Edexcel. Each assignment will have a deadline.

Case study: Getting to grips with assignments

Michelle is thinking about taking a BTEC First in Countryside and Environment at school. At this stage, she is not really sure which career path she wants to take but wants to choose subjects that interest her. During a school options day, Michelle talks to one of the year 11 learners who is currently studying for a BTEC First. She wants to know if the work is hard and how many exams there are in addition to her GCSEs.

"We're taking three units. We get assignments for each unit that are broken down into tasks marked with either pass, merit or distinction. Many of these tasks are completed during lesson times and there's no end-of-course exam. Our tutor gives us clear dates when we need to hand in our work and after marking we get really clear feedback on anything we still have to do.

"We can choose the grade we aim for, so most of us decided on merits. The problem I had was that the distinction tasks looked really interesting to me, so I'm now working towards distinction in all three units, – this is equivalent to an A* GCSE.

"When we started on assignment about estate skills, the first task was to make a presentation on health and safety and environmental legislation. We used books and the internet for research, and even had two guest speakers visit. Both visitors gave us lots of great information, which helped us put our presentations together.

"We watch the other presentations and give feedback using a form our tutor gave us. I was enjoying myself so much that it hardly felt like I was working."

- Getting feedback on work doesn't just have to come from your tutor. Who else could provide feedback on your work?

Getting the most from your BTEC

Getting the most from your BTEC involves several skills, such as using your time effectively and working well with other people. Knowing yourself is also important.

Knowing yourself

How would you describe yourself? Make some notes here.

_____

_____

_____

_____

_____

_____

_____

_____

If you described yourself to someone else, would you be able to sum up your temperament and personality, identify your strengths and weaknesses and list your skills? If not, is it because you've never thought about it or because you honestly don't have a clue?

Learning about yourself is often called self-analysis. You may have already done personality tests or careers profiles. If not, there are many available online. However, the information you gain from these profiles is useless unless you can apply it to what you are doing.

Your personality

Everyone is different. For example, some people:
- like to plan in advance; others prefer to be spontaneous
- love being part of a group; others prefer one or two close friends
- enjoy being the life and soul of the party; others prefer to sit quietly and feel uncomfortable at large social gatherings
- are imaginative and creative; others prefer to deal only with facts
- think carefully about all their options before making a decision; others follow their 'gut instincts' and often let their heart rule their head.

Case study: Harvey's personality

Harvey is excited but a little apprehensive about a taster day his school has arranged with the local college. Next year Harvey will be studying animal care once a week at the college.

Local schools join together for the college courses and Harvey is worried. He is very quiet, he doesn't make friends easily and he has never been the sort of person to fit into a group. If his new tutor puts him in a group of loud, confident learners, he is not sure he would cope.

There are 25 learners on the taster day and Harvey's first impressions are soon made. Some of the group are loud and excitable, others have already started chatting amongst themselves, while Harvey, like a couple of others, sits quietly.

The tutors give the group an introduction to animal care and one of the first things they do is take a tour of the small animal unit. Some of the learners who'd shown confidence early on in the day become very quiet when they enter the reptile and insect house. Harvey is the only person who offers to hold the tarantula and many of the other learners comment on how brave he is. The tutors explain that learners would have different preferences about which animals they would like to work with and ask for a show of hands when they reach each area.

During the taster day, they carry out some group activities which show some of their personalities traits. Harvey finds that he is seen as quiet, well-organised, supportive and confident. His new tutor explains that confidence isn't just being loud and excitable it is also showing that you have knowledge of something and that you are willing to share this with others.

- Think about the areas where you are confident in your chosen land and environment subject. Find out what support you can get to build your confidence in the areas where you are less confident.

TRY THIS ⟶

Imagine one of your friends is describing your best features. What would they say?

Personalities in the workplace

There's a mix of personalities in most workplaces. Some people prefer to work behind the scenes, such as many IT practitioners, who like to concentrate on tasks they enjoy doing. Others love high-profile jobs where they may often be involved in high-pressure situations, such as paramedics and television presenters. Most people fall somewhere between these two extremes.

In any job there will be some aspects that are more appealing and interesting than others. If you have a part-time job you will already know this. The same thing applies to any course you take!

Your personality and your BTEC First course

Understanding your personality means you can identify which parts of your course you are likely to find easy and which more difficult. Working out the aspects you need to develop should be positive. You can also think about how your strengths and weaknesses may affect other people.

- Natural planners find it easier to schedule work for assignments.
- Extroverts like giving presentations and working with others but may overwhelm quieter team members.
- Introverts often prefer to work alone and may be excellent at researching information.

BTEC FACT

All BTEC First courses enable you to develop your personal, learning and thinking skills (**PLTS**), which will help you to meet new challenges more easily. (See page 81.)

Activity: What is your personality type?

1a) Identify your own personality type, either by referring to a personality test you have done recently or by going online and doing a reliable test. Go to page 90 to find out how to access an online test.

Print a summary of the completed test or write a brief description of the results for future reference.

b) Use this information to identify the tasks and personal characteristics that you find easy or difficult.

	Easy	Difficult
Being punctual		
Planning how to do a job		
Working neatly and accurately		
Being well organised		
Having good ideas		
Taking on new challenges		
Being observant		
Working with details		
Being patient		
Coping with criticism		
Dealing with customers		
Making decisions		
Keeping calm under stress		
Using your own initiative		

	Easy	Difficult
Researching facts carefully and accurately		
Solving problems		
Meeting deadlines		
Finding and correcting own errors		
Clearing up after yourself		
Helping other people		
Working as a member of a team		
Being sensitive to the needs of others		
Respecting other people's opinions		
Being tactful and discreet		
Being even-tempered		

2 Which thing from your 'difficult' list do you think you should work on improving first? Start by identifying the benefits you will gain. Then decide how to achieve your goal.

Your knowledge and skills

You already have a great deal of knowledge, as well as practical and personal skills gained at school, at home and at work (if you have a part-time job). Now you need to assess these to identify your strengths and weaknesses.

To do this accurately, try to identify evidence for your knowledge and skills. Obvious examples are:

- previous qualifications
- school reports
- occasions when you have demonstrated particular skills, such as communicating with customers or colleagues in a part-time job.

Part-time jobs give you knowledge and skills in a real work setting.

Activity: Check your skills

1 Score yourself from 1 to 5 for each of the skills in the table below.

1 = I'm very good at this skill.

2 = I'm good but could improve this skill.

3 = This skill is only average and I know that I need to improve it.

4 = I'm weak at this skill and must work hard to improve it.

5 = I've never had the chance to develop this skill.

Enter the score in the column headed 'Score A' and add today's date.

2 Look back at the units and topics you will be studying for your course – you entered them into the chart on page 9. Use this to identify any additional skills that you know are important for your course and add them to the table. Then score yourself for these skills, too.

3 Identify the main skills you will need in order to be successful in your chosen career, and highlight them in the table.

Go back and score yourself against each skill after three, six and nine months. That way you can monitor your progress and check where you need to take action to develop the most important skills you will need.

English and communication skills	Score A	Score B (after three months)	Score C (after six months)	Score D (after nine months)
Test dates:				
Reading and understanding different types of texts and information				
Speaking to other people face to face				
Speaking clearly on the telephone				
Listening carefully				
Writing clearly and concisely				
Presenting information in a logical order				
Summarising information				
Using correct punctuation and spelling				
Joining in a group discussion				
Expressing your own ideas and opinions appropriately				
Persuading other people to do something				
Making an oral presentation and presenting ideas clearly				
ICT skills	Score A	Score B (after three months)	Score C (after six months)	Score D (after nine months)
Test dates:				
Using ICT equipment correctly and safely				
Using a range of software				
Accurate keyboarding				
Proofreading				
Using the internet to find and select appropriate information				
Using ICT equipment to communicate and exchange information				
Producing professional documents which include tables and graphics				
Creating and interpreting spreadsheets				
Using PowerPoint				

Maths and numeracy skills	Score A	Score B (after three months)	Score C (after six months)	Score D (after nine months)
Test dates:				
Carrying out calculations (eg money, time, measurements etc) in a work-related situation				
Estimating amounts				
Understanding and interpreting data in tables, graphs, diagrams and charts				
Comparing prices and identifying best value for money				
Solving routine and non-routine work-related numerical problems				

Case study: Drawing on your skills and experience

Most people who have chosen to work within the land and environment sector have a keen interest in working outdoors, have their own animals or already have experience working within the sector, perhaps in a part-time job.

Hannah has been horse riding at the same yard since she was seven years old. She now owns her own horse, which she keeps at the yard. The owner, Erik, has managed the busy horse yard since finishing college and suggested that maybe she should turn her hobby into a career, like he has. Hannah followed Erik's advice and went to a college open day and signed up for a BTEC First in Horse Care. The college is quite a distance from her home, so she will be staying in its student accommodation; the good news is her horse can come too.

Marcus lives next door to a zoo. He has a keen interest in animals but has never been allowed to have his own pets. He makes up for this by volunteering at the zoo and has worked with a variety of animals, birds, amphibians and insects. Marcus loves to be at the zoo first thing in the morning and last thing at night when the staff are the only ones there. Marcus is going to college to study animal care and the zoo has offered him a work experience placement.

While at school, Fran wanted to work in a clothes shop. She completed her work experience with a florist as it was the only shop in the area taking school work experience placements. However, she found that the two weeks she spent working in the florist shop was the best experience she ever had. She had the chance to go to the flower wholesalers in London – even thought it meant getting up at 3 am. Until then, she didn't know that there were so many different varieties of flowers. Fran soon found out that there are many jobs for qualified florists, ranging from working in large hotels to cruise liners. She feels that she has found her career by accident.

Managing your time

Some people are brilliant at managing their time. They do everything they need to and have time left over for activities they enjoy. Other people complain that they don't know where the time goes.

Which are you? If you need help to manage your time – and most people do – you will find help here.

Why time management is important

- It means you stay in control, get less stressed and don't skip important tasks.
- Some weeks will be peaceful, others will be hectic.
- The amount of homework and assignments you have to do will vary.
- As deadlines approach, time always seems to go faster.
- Some work will need to be done quickly, maybe for the next lesson; other tasks may need to be done over several days or weeks. This needs careful planning.
- You may have several assignments or tasks to complete in a short space of time.
- You want to have a social life.

Avoiding time-wasting

We can all plan to do work, and then find our plans go wrong. There may be several reasons for this. How many of the following do *you* do?

Top time-wasting activities
1 Allowing (or encouraging) people to interrupt you.
2 Not having the information, handouts or textbook you need because you've lost them or lent them to someone else.
3 Chatting to people, making calls or sending texts when you should be working.
4 Getting distracted because you simply must keep checking out MySpace, Facebook or emails.
5 Putting off jobs until they are a total nightmare, then panicking.
6 Daydreaming.
7 Making a mess of something so you have to start all over again.

Planning and getting organised

The first step in managing your time is to plan ahead and be well organised. Some people are naturally good at this. They think ahead, write down their commitments in a diary or planner, and store their notes and handouts neatly and carefully so they can find them quickly.

How good are your working habits?

Talking to friends can take up a lot of time

Improving your planning and organisational skills

1 Use a diary or planner to schedule working times into your weekdays and weekends.

2 Have a place for everything and everything in its place.

3 Be strict with yourself when you start work. If you aren't really in the mood, set a shorter time limit and give yourself a reward when the time is up.

4 Keep a diary in which you write down exactly what work you have to do.

5 Divide up long or complex tasks into manageable chunks and put each 'chunk' in your diary with a deadline of its own.

6 Write a 'to do' list if you have several different tasks. Tick them off as you go.

7 Always allow more time than you think you need for a task.

TRY THIS ➜

Analyse your average day.

How many hours do you spend sleeping, eating, travelling, attending school or college, working and taking part in leisure activities?

How much time is left for homework and assignments?

Case study: Problems managing time

Mika reflects on his decision to turn down a personal tutor at school. "I've always been one of those people who do everything at the last minute. My homework is generally done the night before it's due in. I frequently distract people during lesson time, and I'm not very organised. Like I said everything is last minute and if I forget to do something, I'll just make an excuse to get out of it.'

When Mika started year 11 he was already behind in his BTEC First studies. Most of the other learners were handing in assignments at merit or distinction level. Mika, however, was missing most deadlines and barely scraping a pass. His tutor offered help. At Mika's school there are personal tutors who can help Mika set his action plans, organise his folders and divide his work into manageable chunks.

"I didn't think I needed that kind of help so I turned it down. My friends started getting different, and more interesting work than me. I was getting considerably behind. I kept acting like I didn't care, but really I did. I should've taken help at the start of year 11 so that I could stay on track. Instead, I just kept getting more behind.

"I'm now getting some help for an hour a week. I'm able to keep up with my work and I've even met some deadlines. I'll still only get a pass overall. I know full well I could've got at least a merit if I'd made more effort, but I only have myself to blame."

TOP TIPS

If you become distracted by social networking sites or email when you're working, set yourself a time limit of 10 minutes or so to indulge yourself.

BTEC FACT

If you have serious problems that are interfering with your ability to work or to concentrate, talk to your tutor. There are many ways in which BTEC learners who have personal difficulties can be supported to help them continue with their studies.

Activity: Managing time

1 The correct term for something you do in preference to starting a particular task is a 'displacement activity'. In the workplace this includes things like often going to the water cooler to get a drink, and constantly checking emails and so on online. People who work from home may tidy up, watch television or even cook a meal to put off starting a job.

Write down *your* top three displacement activities.

2 Today is Wednesday. Sajid has several jobs to do tonight and has started well by making a 'to do' list. He's worried that he won't get through all the things on his list and, because he works on Thursday and Friday evenings, that the rest will have to wait until Saturday.

a) Look through Sajid's list and decide which jobs are top priority and *must* be done tonight and which can be left until Saturday if he runs out of time.

b) Sajid is finding that his job is starting to interfere with his ability to do his assignments. What solutions can you suggest to help him?

Jobs to do

– File handouts from today's classes

– Phone Tom (left early today) to tell him the time of our presentation tomorrow has been changed to 11 am

– Research information online for next Tuesday's lesson

– Complete table from rough notes in class today

– Rewrite section of leaflet to talk about at tutorial tomorrow

– Write out class's ideas for the charity of the year, ready for course representatives meeting tomorrow lunchtime

– Redo handout Tom and I are giving out at presentation

– Plan how best to schedule assignment received today – deadline 3 weeks

– Download booklet from website ready for next Monday's class

Getting the most from work experience

On some BTEC First courses, all learners have to do a **work placement**. On others, like the BTEC Level 2 First in Creative Media Production, they are recommended but not essential. If you are doing one, you need to prepare so that you get the most out of it. The checklists in this section will help.

Before you go checklist

1. Find out about the organisation by researching online.

2. Check that you have all the information you'll need about the placement.

3. Check the route you will need to take and how long it will take you. Always allow longer on the first day.

4. Check with your tutor what clothes are suitable and make sure you look the part.

5. Check that you know any rules or guidelines you must follow.

6. Check that you know what to do if you have a serious problem during the placement, such as being too ill to go to work.

7. Talk to your tutor if you have any special personal concerns.

8. Read the unit(s) that relate to your placement carefully. Highlight points you need to remember or refer to regularly.

9. Read the assessment criteria that relate to the unit(s) and use these to make a list of the information and evidence you'll need to obtain.

10. Your tutor will give you an official logbook or diary – or just use a notebook. Make notes each evening while things are fresh in your mind, and keep them safely.

While you're on work placement

Ideally, on your first day you'll be told about the business and what you'll be expected to do. You may even be allocated to one particular member of staff who will be your 'mentor'. However, not all firms operate like this, and if everyone is very busy, your **induction** may be rushed. If so, stay positive and watch other people to see what they're doing. Then offer to help where you can.

BTEC FACT

If you need specific evidence from a work placement for a particular unit, your tutor may give you a logbook or work diary, and will tell you how you will be assessed in relation to the work that you will do.

TRY THIS

You're on work experience. The placement is interesting and related to the job you want to do. However, you've been watching people most of the time and want to get more involved. Identify three jobs you think you could offer to do.

While you're there

1. Arrive with a positive attitude, knowing that you are going to do your best and get the most out of your time there.

2. Although you may be nervous at first, don't let that stop you from smiling at people, saying 'hello' and telling them your name.

3. Arrive punctually – or even early – every day. If you're delayed for any reason, phone and explain. Then get there as soon as you can.

4. If you take your mobile phone, switch it off when you arrive.

5. If you have nothing to do, offer to help someone who is busy or ask if you can watch someone who is doing a job that interests you.

6. Always remember to thank people who give you information, show you something or agree that you can observe them.

7. If you're asked to do something and don't understand what to do, ask for it to be repeated. If it's complicated, write it down.

8. If a task is difficult, start it and then check back that you are doing it correctly before you go any further.

9. Obey all company rules, such as regulations and procedures relating to health and safety and using machinery, the use of IT equipment, and access to confidential information.

10. Don't rush off as fast as you can at the end of the day. Check first with your mentor or supervisor whether you can leave.

TOP TIPS

Observing people who are skilled at what they do helps you learn a lot, and may even be part of your **assignment brief.**

Coping with problems

Problems are rare but can happen. The most common ones are being bored because you're not given any work to do or upset because you feel someone is treating you unfairly. Normally, the best first step is to talk to your mentor at work or your supervisor. However, if you're very worried or upset, you may prefer to get in touch with your tutor instead – do it promptly.

Getting experience of work in the land and environment sector

One of the best experiences while studying can come from work experience. Local businesses are usually more than happy to give placements to keen and enthusiastic learners.

It is important to remember that some jobs within the land and environment sector may need previous experience, or may have strict health and safety requirements. This may limit the kind of work you can undertake.

Case study: Diego finds a work placement

Diego has been struggling to find a work placement in farming so he asks his tutor for help. Agriculture is not a 9 to 5 activity, but Diego relies on public transport, which narrows down where he can apply.

Diego's tutor discusses a residential work placement with him and his parents. She explains that he would be able to get a real taste for working in his chosen area and that she can arrange an interview at a dairy farm located 30 miles away. Diego and his parents have their concerns, but in general feel it would be a fabulous opportunity.

"I was really excited heading for the interview with my tutor. Steve, the owner, was ready to greet us and took us to his office for a chat.

He was very welcoming. He asked what I knew about dairy farming. I had to be truthful and say not much at all. I think my honesty went down well and, after several more questions, Steve offered me a placement.

"Steve explained there would be jobs I would not be able to do due to strict health and safety rules, but also reassured me that there would be plenty of variety during my time with him. I would be getting up at 3.30 am, ready to start work, milking, at 4 am. We would then spend the rest of the morning cleaning and feeding. I would also be shown how to complete paperwork and help out in the farm shop where the public can buy fresh dairy products. I cannot wait to start."

Activity: Finding work experience in the land and environment industry

It is important to remember that your centre will not be the only one in the area with learners looking for placements, so the earlier you apply the better chance you have of getting a placement. Make a note below of your work experience dates so that, with help from your centre, you can start organising your search for a placement.

My work experience dates are:

Using directories, newspapers, and the internet, and getting advice from your tutor, start making a list of possible work placements available to you. Use the space over the page to record your findings.

Several things will need to be considered when deciding on where to apply for a work experience placement. For example, you need to consider how you will get to the job, particularly if you are required to be at work very late or very early in the day.

Things to consider	What shall I do about it?

During or shortly after your work placement, complete a needs analysis to help you and your tutor talk through some of your thoughts and feelings about your experience. You can use the table below to capture some of the information you will need to discuss.

Your needs	Your concerns	Your expectations

Working with other people

Everyone finds it easy to work with people they like and far harder with those they don't. On your course you'll often be expected to work as a team to do a task. This gives you practice in working with different people.

You will be expected to:

- contribute to the task
- listen to other people's views
- adapt to other people's ways of working
- take responsibility for your own contribution
- agree the best way to resolve any problems.

BTEC FACT

An important part of your BTEC course is learning how to work positively and productively with other people.

These are quite complex skills. It helps if you understand the benefits to be gained by working cooperatively with other people and know the best way to achieve this.

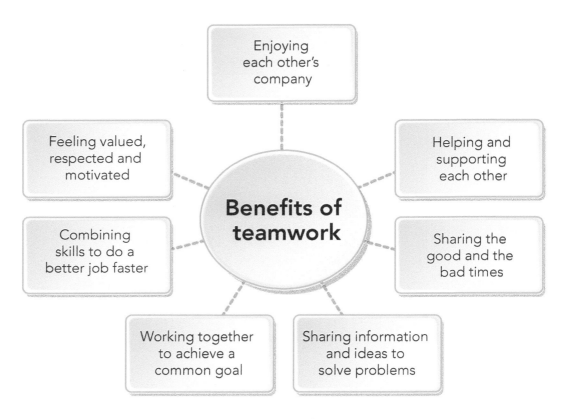

The benefits of good working relationships and teamwork

Case study: Working as a team

Sabrina's class has been given a new assignment – designing a garden for the Chelsea Flower Show. They are told to work as a team to come up with a winning design. The team has eight weeks to produce a design that will be assessed by a panel of judges.

Everyone starts to come up with ideas individually and works hard on their own designs. Some great ideas begin to surface. Nonetheless, the tutor can see there are about to be problems, but decides to take a back seat and wait to see what happens.

Everyone gathers round with their sketches. It soon becomes apparent that there are hugely different designs. One learner favours the wild garden look, while another likes sharp lines and bold colours. Other designs include a garden built by using recycled materials, a child-friendly garden and a water garden. The designs are so diverse that nothing fits together. Arguments

start to develop, as each learner thinks that they have produced the best design.

The tutor explains that they have missed the first vital instruction of the task, which was to work as a team. He also explains that if they don't organise themselves into a team early on, then the project will be a disaster. They agree with him and decide to start again from scratch.

Sabrina suggests that they have an initial meeting to assign different responsibilities to people and to set some ground rules. She also thinks it will be a good idea to take minutes so that everyone can keep track of their individual responsibilities. Her tutor thinks this is a great idea and suggests they meet weekly. To give the project a better chance of success, he also gives them guidance on budgeting, schedules (by setting deadlines and knowing how long things might take to do), sponsorship, travel arrangements and appointing a team leader.

Golden rules for everyone (including the team leader!)

The secret of a successful team is that everyone works together. The role of the team leader is to make this as easy as possible by listening to people's views and coordinating everyone's efforts. A team leader is not there to give orders.

Can you imagine how disorganised a zoo would be if its staff didn't work as a team? Animals might not be fed or exercised, and they could be left in dirty cages. The success of any zoo business depends on teamwork; from opening the gate to let the public in, to letting the animals out in the open for them to be seen. Everyone has their own role and responsibilities to carry out for the effective and efficient running of the zoo. As a team member, you are also in a supportive role. This means that if someone is struggling, you are there to lend a hand.

It is important to keep in mind that teams cannot achieve their goals without the hard work and commitment of all its members. Use the table below to record three golden rules for being a good team member.

Three golden rules for being a good team member
1.
2.
3.

A good team leader is essential for the team to succeed; the leader will take a lead role in ensuring tasks are achieved. This can be a difficult role in a class situation, especially if the team leader is not everyone's first choice.

If you are the team leader, there may be times when you do not agree with some decisions being made within your team, or others may not agree with you. Use the table below to show the three golden rules you would use to ensure that all team members feel valued.

Three golden rules for ensuring team members feel valued
1.
2.
3.

Positive teamwork checklist

- ✔ Be loyal to your team, including the team leader.
- ✔ Be reliable and dependable at all times.
- ✔ Be polite. Remember to say 'please' and 'thank you'.
- ✔ Think before you speak.
- ✔ Treat everyone the same.
- ✔ Make allowances for individual personalities. Give people 'space' if they need it, but be ready to offer support if they ask for it.
- ✔ Admit mistakes and apologise if you've done something wrong – learn from it but don't dwell on it.
- ✔ Give praise when it's due, give help when you can, and thank people who help you.
- ✔ Keep confidences, and any promises that you make.

TRY THIS

Work out whether you're usually passive, assertive or aggressive when you're annoyed. You've arranged to meet Sam to see a film. He arrives 20 minutes late.

Do you:

a) shrug and say nothing in case he gets upset

b) ask why he didn't text you to give you warning

c) say that it's the last time you'll ever go anywhere with him and walk off?

Which do you think would be the most effective – and why?

In the planning stages of a project, it is often how things are said that will

There are many benefits to be gained from working as a team.

cause problems within a group. Keeping calm and not being personal with comments will ensure that issues can be dealt with in a constructive manner.

Look at the comments in the table below and see if you can rephrase what has been said to make it sound more constructive.

What was said	How could this have been said?
Why should we always do what you want?	
You're only doing the planning because I don't want to	
We all think that's a stupid idea	
I can afford it; money is no issue to me	

Getting the most from special events

BTEC First courses usually include several practical activities and special events. These enable you to find out information, develop your skills and knowledge in new situations, and enjoy new experiences. They may include visits to external venues, visits from specialist speakers, and team events.

Most learners enjoy the chance to do something different. You'll probably look forward to some events more than others. If you're ready to get actively involved, you'll usually gain the most benefit. It also helps to make a few preparations!

Case study: Getting the most from a visit to a royal estate

Shaun is preparing for his class trip to a royal estate. The trip has been arranged by his tutor to help the class complete an assignment for the unit on estate skills. The tutor briefs the class beforehand to look at the assignment criteria so that they can prepare and ask relevant questions.

Shaun and his friend Olli have decided to work as a pair. They look through the assignment together and come up with these questions.

- How large is the estate?
- How do you plan estate maintenance work?
- Why is it important to plan the estate maintenance?
- What problems could arise?

- What qualifications do you need to work here?
- How many staff do you have?
- How do you make sure health and safety regulations are met?
- Do you have an environmental policy?

After completing their questions, Shaun looks up the estate on the internet and finds the answer to the first question. Olli visits the local tourist information centre and picks up a leaflet on the royal estate. He finds the estate's environmental policy is written on the back of the leaflet. Shaun and Olli also now have a map for their walk round the estate.

Being prepared for a visit means you get much more out of it.

Special events checklist

✔ Check you understand how the event relates to your course.

✔ If a visit or trip is not something you would normally find very interesting, try to keep an open mind. You might get a surprise!

✔ Find out what you're expected to do, and any rules or guidelines you must follow, including about your clothes or appearance.

✔ Always allow enough time to arrive five minutes early, and make sure you're never late.

✔ On an external visit, make notes on what you see and hear. This is essential if you have to write about it afterwards, use your information to answer questions in an assignment or do something practical.

✔ If an external speaker is going to talk to your class, prepare a list of questions in advance. Nominate someone to thank the speaker afterwards. If you want to record the talk, it's polite to ask first.

✔ For a team event, you may be involved in planning and helping to allocate different team roles. You'll be expected to participate positively in any discussions, to talk for some (but not all) of the time, and perhaps to volunteer for some jobs yourself.

✔ Write up any notes you make as soon as you can – while you can still understand what you wrote!

TRY THIS

At the last minute, you're asked to propose a vote of thanks to a visiting speaker on behalf of your class. What would you say?

A visiting speaker may provide day-to-day details about working life that can't be found in books.

Activity: A day in the life of a groom

Russell is a full-time groom in stables owned by a famous rider. He agrees to talk to BTEC First learners about his job role. He decides to talk them through his average working day and answer any questions they may have.

Use the space below to record your thoughts about what you might ask someone in a job role you're interested in.

_____

_____

_____

_____

Russell explains his average working day to the BTEC First learners using a chart. Use the blank chart to show what some of your responsibilities might be in the job you would like to do.

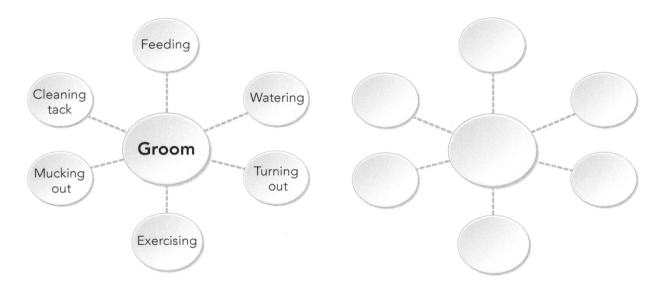

What are the benefits of meeting someone who works in the industry rather than researching the role in books or on the internet?

_____

_____

_____

Resources and research

Understanding resources

Resources are items that help you do something. The most obvious one is money! To obtain your BTEC First award, however, your resources are rather different.

Different kinds of resources

Physical resources

Physical resources are things like textbooks, computers and any specialist equipment.

- Popular textbooks, laptops for home use and specialist equipment may need to be booked. Leaving it until the last minute is risky.
- You can ask for help if you don't know how to use resources properly.
- You should check what stationery and equipment you need at the start of your course and make sure you have it.
- You need to look after your resources carefully. This saves money and time spent replacing lost items.

People as resources

There are many people who can help you through your course:
- family members who help and support you
- your tutor

○ friends in your group who collect handouts for you and phone you to keep you up to date when you're absent

○ librarians and computer technicians at your centre or your local library

○ expert practitioners.

Expert practitioners

Expert practitioners have worked hard to be successful in their chosen area. They have the skills and knowledge needed to do the job properly. They can be invaluable when you're researching information (see page 47). You can also learn a lot by watching them at work, especially if you can ask them questions about what they do, what they find hard, and any difficulties they've had.

A professional florist may be a useful source of information if you are taking the BTEC Level 2 First in Floristry.

Try to observe more than one expert practitioner:

○ It gives you a better picture about what they do.

○ No single job will cover all aspects of work that might apply to your studies.

○ You may find some experts more approachable and easy to understand than others. For example, if someone is impatient because they're busy it may be difficult to ask them questions, or if someone works very quickly you may find it hard to follow what they're doing.

If you have problems, just note what you've learned and compare it with your other observations. And there's always the chance that you're observing someone who's not very good at their job! You'll only know this for certain if you've seen what people should be doing.

Activity: Create your own resource list

There are many different ways for you to carry out research, some of which you will enjoy doing more than others. Using a diverse range of information sources allows you to develop your sector knowledge and complete your assignments effectively.

Textbooks

There are an enormous number of textbooks that have been written for the land and environment sector to support you with your BTEC First studies. You will be given guidance about those that cover the units you are studying. Some textbooks contain useful activities and projects that you can complete in your own time to further develop your knowledge and understanding.

Newspapers and magazines

There are many specialist trade newspapers and magazines that carry up-to-date information about the land and environment sector. Your school or college might subscribe to these publications. If not, many offer student discounts if you subscribe while you are studying.

Television

Numerous television documentaries cover nature and the environment, gardening and animals. Watching some of these programmes can be very helpful. Fly-on-the-wall programmes follow real people doing real jobs in the land and environment sectors. These will not just help you with your course work but may also give you an insight into your career options.

Internet

The internet opens up a whole world of useful information. You can use it to find out about anything and everything. Most larger companies will have their own websites where you can find really useful information about a company, from its location to the organisation of its departments.

People

People can be one of your best information resources. Someone's actual experiences can offer a different point of view that may help you, for example, when you need to evaluate methods of doing something or assess the value of carrying out a certain procedure.

Leaflets

Tourist leaflets can give useful information when you are researching zoos, aquariums, rescue centres, estates, stately homes, stud farms, fishing lakes, markets, parks and gardens.

Catalogues and brochures

Despite the excellent internet resources that are now available, being able to have a catalogue in front of you is often a much easier information source than using a website. You can easily research up-to-date equipment and materials, and quickly find prices and product descriptions.

Stationery

Make sure that you are prepared for your lessons. You will need pens, pencils, paper and a file to store handouts, notes, assignment briefs and work you complete for homework tasks. A small note book that can fit into your pocket is also essential for those times when you need to take notes during practical, outdoor tasks.

Create your resource list using the grid below. Look at the suggested resources in the unit specifications to help you.

Library-based resources: such as textbooks, newspapers and magazines, leaflets and brochures	
Internet-based resources: such as websites and online catalogues	
People and businesses: such as employers, friends, tutors	
Stationery: such as pens, paper, file, notebook	

Finding the information you need

The information explosion

There are lots of different ways to find out information – books, newspapers, magazines, television, radio, CDs, DVDs, the internet. And you can exchange information with other people by texting, sending an email or phoning someone.

All this makes it much easier to obtain information. If you know what you're doing, you can probably find most of what you need sitting at a computer. But there are some dangers.

- Finding exactly what you want online takes skill. You need to know what you're doing.
- It's easy to get too much information and become overwhelmed.
- It's unlikely that everything you need will be available online.
- The information you read may be out of date.
- The information may be neither reliable nor true.

Define what you are trying to find. (The more precise you are, the more likely you are to find what you're looking for.)

Know where to look for it. (Remember: the internet is not the only source of information.)

Recognise when you have found appropriate information.

Know what to do with information once you've found it. (Make sure that you understand it, interpret it correctly and record the source where you found it.)

Know when to stop looking (especially if you have a deadline).

Finding and using information effectively

Before you start

There are four things that will help you look in the right place and target your search properly.

Ask yourself ...	Because ...	Example
Exactly what do I need to find out?	It will save you time and effort.	If you need information about accidents, you need to know what type of accident and over what time period.
Why do I need this information and who is going to read it?	This puts the task into context. You need to identify the best type of information to obtain and how to get it.	If you're making a poster or leaflet for children, you'll need simple information that can be presented in a graphical format. If, however, you're giving a workplace presentation on accidents, you'll need tables and graphs to illustrate your talk.
Where can I find it?	You need to consider whether your source is trustworthy and up to date. The internet is great, but you must check that the sites you use are reliable.	To find out about accidents in the workplace you could talk to the health and safety at work officer. To find examples of accidents in your local area you could look through back copies of your local newspaper in the local library or newspaper offices.
What is my deadline?	You know how long you have to find the information and use it.	

Your three main sources of information are:

- libraries or learning resource centres
- the internet
- asking other people, for example through interviews and questionnaires.

Researching in libraries

You can use the learning resource centre in your school or college, or a local public library. Public libraries usually have a large reference section with many resources available for loan, including CD-ROMs, encyclopaedias, government statistics, magazines, journals and newspapers, and databases such as Infotrac, which contains articles from newspapers and magazines over the last five years.

The librarian will show you how to find the resources you need and how to look up a specific book (or author) to check if it is available or is out on loan.

TRY THIS

Schedule your research time by calculating backwards from the deadline date. Split the time you have 50/50 between searching for information and using it. This stops you searching for too long and getting lots of interesting material, but then not having the time to use it properly!

Some books and resources can only be used in the library itself, while others can be taken out on short-term or long-term loan. You need to plan how to access and use the resources that are popular or restricted.

Using your library

✔ If your centre has an intranet you might be able to check which books and CD-ROMs are available without actually visiting the library.

✔ All libraries have photocopying facilities, so take enough change with you to copy articles that you can't remove. Write down the source of any article you photocopy, ie the name and the date of the publication.

✔ Learn how to keep a reference file (or bibliography) in which you store the details of all your sources and references. A bibliography must include CDs, DVDs and other information formats, not just books and magazines.

✔ If your search is complicated, go at a quiet time when the librarian can help you.

✔ Don't get carried away if you find several books that contain the information you need. Too many can be confusing.

✔ Use the index to find information quickly by searching for key words. Scan the index using several likely alternatives.

✔ Only use books that you find easy to understand. A book is only helpful if you can retell the information in your own words.

Researching online

A good search engine such as Google will help you find useful websites. They look for sites based on the information you enter in the search box. In some cases, such as Ask.co.uk, you may get the chance to refine your choice after entering your key words or question.

Finding information on a website

Wikipedia is a popular free online encyclopaedia. It has been criticised because entries may be inaccurate as members of the public can edit the site. However, Wikipedia is trying to prevent this by organising professional editing.

If you're not sure whether something you read is correct, or if there is anything strange about it, check it against information on another site. Make sure you ask your tutor's opinion, too.

With large websites, it can be difficult to find what you need. Always read the whole screen – there may be several menus in different parts of the screen.

To help you search, many large websites have:
- their own search facility or a site map that lists site content with links to the different pages
- links to similar sites where you might find more information. Clicking a link should open a new window, so you'll still be connected to the original site.

TRY THIS

Search engines don't just find websites. On Google, the options at the top of your screen include 'images', 'news' and 'maps'. If you click on 'more' and then 'even more', you'll find other options, too. You'll usually find the most relevant information if you use the UK version of a search engine. Only search the whole web if you deliberately want to include European and American information. Go to page 90 to find out how you can see this in action.

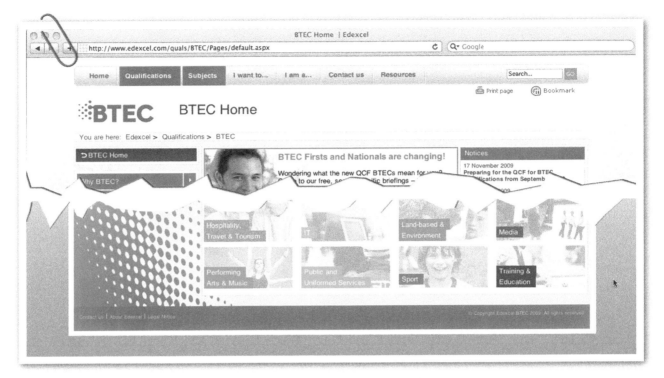

There may be useful information and links at the top, foot or either side of a web page.

There are several other useful sites you could visit when researching online.

○ **Directory sites** show websites in specific categories so you can focus your search at the start.

○ **Forums** are sites, or areas of a website, where people post comments on an issue. They can be useful if you want to find out opinions on a topic. You can usually read them without registering.

○ **News sites** include the BBC website as well as the sites for all the daily newspapers. Check the website of your local newspaper, too.

Printing information

○ Only print information that you're sure will be useful. It's easy to print too much and find yourself drowning in paper.

○ Make quick notes on your print-outs so that you remember why you wanted them. It will jog your memory when you're sorting through them later.

○ If there's a printer-friendly option, use it. It will give you a print-out without unnecessary graphics or adverts.

○ Check the bottom line of your print-outs. It should show the URL for that page of the website, and the date. You need those if you have to list your sources or if you want to quote from the page.

TRY THIS

Go to page 90 to find out how to access a website where you can see how directory sites work.

TOP TIPS

Bookmark sites you use regularly by adding the URL to your browser. How to do this will depend on which browser you use, such as Internet Explorer, Firefox.

Researching by asking other people

You're likely to do this for two reasons:
- you need help from someone who knows a lot about a topic
- you need to find out several people's opinions on something.

Information from an expert

Explain politely why you are carrying out the investigation. Ask questions slowly and clearly about what they do and how they do it. If they don't mind, you could take written notes so you remember what they tell you. Put the name and title of the person, and the date, at the top. This is especially important if you might be seeing more than one person, to avoid getting your notes muddled up.

Ask whether you may contact them again, in case there's anything you need to check. Write down their phone number or email address. Above all, remember to say thank you.

Case study: Using other people as a resource for your research

Kimona needs to research health and safety regulations and safe working practices for her BTEC First. She has already used books and the internet, but is very confused as there is such a lot of information that she has not understood.

She goes back to her resource list and then remembers about using other people as a research tool. A while back, during her induction, Kimona had met the school's health and safety officer. She decides to book an appointment with him through her tutor.

Using the unit specification to help her, Kimona puts together a list of the things she wants to ask about. Her list includes:

- health and safety legislation
- health and safety codes of practice

- the employer's responsibilities
- the employee's responsibilities
- safe working practice examples
- who writes these documents
- risk assessments.

Meeting the health and safety officer proves very valuable to Kimona. She is able to ask him many questions relevant to her assignment – and have the answers explained in a way that she understands. He shows her clear examples of risk assessments and gives her a template to use when completing her own assessments. Kimona finds that, with the school health and safety officer's help, she can now do her own risk assessments.

- Think about where else in your course it might be useful to use people as a research tool.

The opinions of several people

The easiest way to do this is with a questionnaire. You can either give people the questionnaire to complete themselves, or interview them and complete it yourself. Professional interviewers often telephone people to ask questions, but at this stage it's not a good idea unless you know the people you're phoning and they're happy for you to do this.

Devising a questionnaire

1 Make sure it has a title and clear instructions.

2 Rather than ask for opinions, give people options, eg yes/no, maybe/always, never/sometimes. This will make it easier to analyse the results.

3 Or you can ask interviewees to give a score, say out of 5, making it clear what each number represents, eg 5 = excellent, 3 = very good.

4 Keep your questionnaire short so that your interviewees don't lose interest. Between 10 and 15 questions is probably about right, as long as that's enough to find out all you need.

5 Remember to add 'thank you' at the end.

6 Decide upon the representative sample of people you will approach. These are the people whose views are the most relevant to the topic you're investigating.

7 Decide how many responses you need to get a valid answer. This means that the answer is representative of the wider population. For example, if you want views on food in your canteen, it's pointless only asking five people. You might pick the only five people who detest (or love) the food it serves.

TOP TIPS

Design your questionnaire so that you get quantifiable answers. This means you can easily add them up to get your final result.

TRY THIS

Always test your draft questionnaire on several people, to highlight any confusing questions or instructions.

Questionnaires can be a very useful source of research

Activity: Referencing your assignments

When completing your assignments it will be necessary to reference where you found your information. The easiest way to do this is to keep a note of it as you go along. Try creating a blank table with headings so that you can make notes as you work. This can be typed up neatly at the end of your assignment to hand in to your tutor.

Remember to use as wide a range of research tools as possible. Keep a note of this useful information in your table too; you may be able to reference some of it within your work. Throughout your course you may be given useful advice and guidance from all sorts of people such as your peers, tutors, support staff, employers, colleagues and family, this all needs referencing, too.

Source	Date and where found	Note of information gathered	Useful comments
Example: Book The Tree and Shrub Expert, by Dr DG Hessayon	23/09/10 Page 123	Grower's Dictionary	Plant definitions to help with Unit 4
Example: Website www.hse.gov.uk	1/10/10 About HSE link – legislation link	Health and safety legislation – workers' rights	Your rights and responsibilities, good guidance on your duty of care for Unit 6

Use the blank table on the following page to record information you find out about the personal protective equipment (PPE) you will need for your course. Use at least three different sources of information.

Source	Date and where found	Note of information gathered	Useful comments

Managing your information

Whether you've found lots of information or only a little, assessing what you have and using it wisely is very important. This section will help you avoid the main pitfalls.

Organising and selecting your information

Organising your information

The first step is to organise your information so that it's easy to use.

- Make sure your written notes are neat and have a clear heading – it's often useful to date them, too.
- Note useful pages in any books or magazines you have borrowed.
- Highlight relevant parts of any handouts or leaflets.
- Work out the results of any questionnaires you've used.

Activity: Organising your information

It is often difficult to know how best to cover everything in your assignments. However, you will be given clear well-laid out assignment briefs that have all the relevant information you need. To stay on track, and ensure you have covered everything that is being asked of you, try creating your own check sheets. You could create a table on your computer to ensure you have fully covered the assignment requirements in the correct format. Lastly, your table can be used as a final check sheet for compiling your information to hand in on the due date.

For this example, let's look at *Unit 1: Undertake Work Related Experience in the Land-based Industries* from the BTEC First in Agriculture. You must describe different types of jobs within a land and environment industry. To meet the grading criteria, you are required to include things such as the job description, as well as essential and desirable personal requirements. Complete the tableon the following page, using newspapers or magazines to help you.

Job title	Job description/role	Essential requirements	Desirable requirements

By producing a check list in table format you can see at a glance what needs to be addressed. This helps you to focus your research. Notes can be typed or written into boxes and extended into a description when sufficient information has been found.

Selecting your information

Re-read the **assignment brief** or instructions you were given, to remind yourself of the exact wording of the question(s) and divide your information into three groups.

1 Information that is totally relevant.

2 Information that is not as good, but could come in useful.

3 Information that doesn't match the questions or assignment brief very much but that you kept because you couldn't find anything better!

Check there are no obvious gaps in your information against the questions or assignment brief. If there are, make a note of them so that you know exactly what you still have to find. Although it's ideal to have everything you need before you start work, don't delay if you're short of time.

Putting your information in order

Putting your information in a logical order means you can find what you want easily. It will save you time in the long run. This is doubly important if you have lots of information and will be doing the work over several sessions.

File management

Organisational skills are very important when you are studying. Spending time managing your files will mean you are able to find things easily when you need them. There is nothing more frustrating than losing something you know you had.

Use dividers in your files to keep your work in sections. For example, each of your units can be organised into separate section. You can use these sections to file your assignment briefs, handouts, research and anything else relevant to the unit. Have blank sheets of paper in each section and use table templates to take notes effectively.

Your assignment timetable can be taped into the front of your file so important dates for reviews or handing in assignments are not missed.

Case study: Ali and Henry help each other

Henry is very disorganised, he can never find paperwork he has been given and he is always in a muddle when it comes to writing his assignments. Ali, on the other hand, is much more organised. His folders are neatly kept and his work is divided up so that he can find things easily. Their tutor suggests that Ali could help Henry to organise his work.

"When I saw Henry's bag it looked like something you would take to a recycling plant," says Ali. "I was more than happy to help. We started by emptying everything out of his file. There were dividers in amongst the work, so we started with those."

Ali helps Henry sort his work into piles. Each pile represented a unit which could then be divided into sections. They label plastic wallets for each section: assignments, handouts, notes. Before long Henry's folder looks like Ali's.

While organising Henry's work Ali notices how Henry takes notes in lessons. Ali has always struggled in this area and is always losing track of what the tutor is saying.

"It's easy," explains Henry. "I use shapes. The main topic we're discussing goes at the top in a circle and then I add smaller circles or boxes which branch off to jot down the main points. I find this easier as it reminds me what we are discussing so I can do extra research later. This sort of diagram is called a graphical organiser – although some people call it a tree diagram, cloud bursts or thought showers."

Interpreting and presenting your information

The next stage is to use your information to prepare the document and/or oral presentation you have to give. There are four steps.

1 Understand what you're reading.

2 Interpret what you're reading.

3 Know the best form in which to produce the information, bearing in mind the purpose for which it is required.

4 Create the required document so that it's in a suitable layout with correct spelling and punctuation.

Understanding what you read

As a general rule, never use information that you don't understand. However, nobody understands complex or unfamiliar material the first time they read it, especially if they just scan through it quickly. Before you reject it, try this:

Read it once to get the main idea.

Read it again, slowly, to try to take in more detail.

Look up any words you don't know in a dictionary to find out what they mean.

Write your own version.

Summarise the main points in your own words.

Read it a third time and underline or highlight the main points. (If this is a book or magazine that you shouldn't write in, take a photocopy first and write on that.)

Special note: Show both the article and your own version to your tutor to check your understanding. This will help you identify any points you missed out and help you improve your skills of interpreting and summarising.

Understanding unfamiliar information

BTEC FACT

In your assignments, it's better to separate opinions from facts. If you're quoting someone's views, make this clear. (See also page 56.)

Interpreting what you read

Interpreting what you read is different from understanding it. This is because you can't always take it for granted that something you read means what it says. The writer may have had a very strong or biased opinion, or may have exaggerated for effect. This doesn't mean that you can't use the information.

Strong opinions and bias

People often have strong points of view about certain topics. This may be based on reliable facts, but not always! We can all jump to conclusions that may not be very logical, especially if we feel strongly about something.

Things aren't always what they seem to be. Are these boys fighting or are they having a good time?

Exaggeration

Many newspapers exaggerate facts to startle and attract their readers.

LOCAL FIRM DOUBLES STAFF IN TWO WEEKS!

This newspaper headline sounds very positive. You could easily think it means employment is growing and there are more jobs in your area. Then you read on, and find the firm had only four staff and now has eight!

Tables and graphs

You need to be able to interpret what the figures mean, especially when you look at differences between columns or rows. For example, your friend might have an impressive spreadsheet that lists his income and expenditure. In reality, it doesn't tell you much until you add the figures up and subtract one from the other. Only then can you say whether he is getting into debt. And even if he is, you need to see his budget over a few months, rather than just one which may be exceptional.

Choosing a format

You may have been given specific instructions about the format and layout of a document you have to produce, in which case life is easy as long as you follow them! If not, think carefully about the best way to set out your information so that it is clear.

TRY THIS

There are many scare stories in the media about issues such as immigration, children's reading ability or obesity. Next time you're watching television and these are discussed, see if you can spot biased views, exaggeration and claims without any supporting evidence.

TOP TIPS

Never make assumptions or jump to conclusions. Make sure you have all the evidence to support your views.

Different formats	Example
text	when you write in paragraphs or prepare a report or summary
graphical	a diagram, graph or chart
pictorial	a drawing, photograph, cartoon or pictogram
tabular	numerical information in a table

The best method(s) will depend on the information you have, the source(s) of your material and the purpose of the document – a leaflet for schoolchildren needs graphics and pictures to make it lively, whereas a report to company shareholders would be mainly in text form with just one or two graphs.

Stating your sources

Whatever format you use, if you are including other people's views, comments or opinions, or copying a table or diagram from another publication, you must state the source by including the name of the author, publication or the web address. This can be in the text or as part of a list at the end. Failure to do this (so you are really pretending other people's work is your own) is known as **plagiarism**. It is a serious offence with penalties to match.

Text format

Creating written documents gets easier with practice. These points should help.

TOP TIPS

Don't just rely on your spellchecker. It won't find a word spelled wrongly that makes another valid word (eg from/form), so you must proofread everything. And remember to check whether it is set to check American English or British English. There are some spelling differences.

Golden rules for written documents

1 Think about who will be reading it, then write in an appropriate language and style.

2 Ensure it is technically correct, ie no wrong spellings or bad punctuation.

3 Take time to make it look good, with clear headings, consistent spacing and plenty of white space.

4 Write in paragraphs, each with a different theme. Leave a line space between each one.

5 If you have a lot of separate points to mention, use bullets or numbered points. Numbered points show a certain order or quantity (step 1, step 2, etc). Use bullet points when there is no suggested order.

6 Only use words that you understand the meaning of, or it might look as if you don't know what you mean.

7 Structure your document so that it has a beginning, middle and end.

8 Prepare a draft and ask your tutor to confirm you are on the right track and are using your information in the best way.

Graphical format

Most people find graphics better than a long description for creating a quick picture in the viewer's mind. There are several types of graphical format, and you can easily produce any of these if you have good ICT skills.

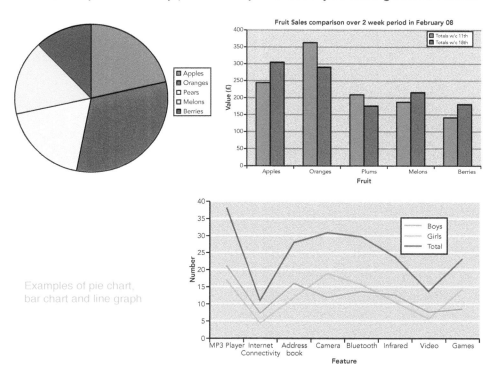

Examples of pie chart, bar chart and line graph

Pictorial format

Newspapers and magazines use pictures to illustrate situations and reduce the amount of words needed. It doesn't always have to be photographs though. For example, a new building may be sketched to show what it will look like.

A pictogram or pictograph is another type of pictorial format, such as charts which use the image of an object (fruit, coins, even pizzas) to represent data, such as the number eaten or amount spent.

Tabular format

A table can be an easy way to communicate information. Imagine a retailer preparing information about the items in stock. Text would be difficult to understand, and comparisons between stock levels and sales would be almost impossible to make. A table, however, would easily show the fastest-selling items.

Tables are also ideal if you are showing rankings – such as best-selling music or books.

Bestsellers list – September 2009

Position	Title	Author	Imprint	Publication
1 (New)	Lost Symbol, The	Brown, Dan	Bantam Press	15-Sep-2009
2 (1)	Complaints, The	Rankin, Ian	Orion	03-Sep-2009
3 (New)	Return Journey, The	Binchy, Maeve	Orion	17-Sep-2009
4 (7)	Sapphire	Price, Katie	Century	30-Jul-2009
5 (9)	Wolf Hall	Mantel, Hilary	Fourth Estate	30-Apr-2009
6 (3)	Week in December, A	Faulks, Sebastian	Hutchinson	03-Sep-2009
7 (2	Alex Cross's Trial	Patterson, James	Century	10-Sep-2009
8 (4)	White Queen, The	Gregory, Philippa	Simon & Schuster Ltd	18-Aug-2009
9 (5)	Even Money	Francis, Dick & Francis, Felix	Michael Joseph	03-Sep-2009
10 (8)	206 Bones	Reichs, Kathy	William Heinemann	27-Aug-2009

National newspaper circulation – September 2009

	August 2009	August 2008	% change on last year	August 09 (without bulks)	March 2009 – August 2009	% change on last year
Sun	3,128,501	3,148,792	-0.64	3,128,501	3,052,480	-2.25
Daily Mail	2,171,686	2,258,843	-3.86	2,044,079	2,178,462	-4.45
Daily Mirror	1,324,883	1,455,270	-8.96	1,324,883	1,331,108	9.44
Daily Star	886,814	751,494	18.01	886,814	855,511	16.65
The Daily Telegraph	814,087	860,298	-5.37	722,644	807,328	-6.73
Daily Express	730,234	748,664	-2.46	730,234	727,824	-1.32
Times	576,185	612,779	-5.97	529,746	588,471	-4.63
Financial Times	395,845	417,570	-5.2	365,269	411,098	-6.7
Daily Record	347,302	390,197	-10.99	345,277	350,306	-10.59
Guardian	311,387	332,587	-6.37	311,387	332,790	-4.11
Independent	187,837	230,033	-18.34	148,551	198,445	-16.76

Activity: Interpreting and presenting your information

Throughout your studies you will be required to present your work in many different formats. Using the scale below rate each of the formats in terms of your confidence to complete them.

Format	Confident ⟶ Not Confident				
	1	2	3	4	5
Word documents: reports, essays etc.					
Publisher: posters, leaflets etc.					
PowerPoint: presentations					
Writing: filling in workbooks					
Tabular: displaying data, especially rankings					
Charts or graphs: displaying data					
Note taking: from reference texts, in lessons					

Which format do you prefer? It will be useful to look back at this table at the end of your course to see how things have changed.

Your assignments will include many different activities to stretch your learning and inspire you to do your best. A common form of assessing your work in land and environment studies is through being observed carrying out specified practical tasks. In your assignment briefs, your tutor will give you clear guidance on the criteria you need to meet for a practical observation. Thinking about what might be needed, pick a practical activity from this list:

- preparing foliage
- feeding rodents
- mucking out a stable
- weeding a boarder
- transporting tools and equipment
- collecting water samples
- reversing a tractor.

Now write down the task you have chosen from list and then note what you think your tutor may be looking for when you are being observed performing this task.

Task:

Observation:

Making presentations

Presentations help you to learn communication skills.

Some people hate the idea of standing up to speak in front of an audience. This is quite normal, and you can use the extra energy from nerves to improve your performance.

Presentations aren't some form of torture devised by your tutor! They are included in your course because they help you learn many skills, such as speaking in public and preparing visual aids. They also help you practise working as a team member, and give you a practical reason for researching information. And it can be far more enjoyable to talk about what you've found out rather than write about it!

There's a knack to preparing and giving a presentation so that you use your energies well, don't waste time, don't fall out with everyone around you and keep your stress levels as low as possible. Think about the task in three stages: preparation, organisation and delivery.

Preparation

Start your initial preparations as soon as you can. Putting them off will only cause problems later. Discuss the task in your team so that everyone is clear about what has to be done and how long you have to do it in.

Divide any research fairly among the team, allowing for people's strengths and weaknesses. You'll also need to agree:

○ which visual aids would be best

○ which handouts you need and who should prepare them

○ where and when the presentation will be held, and what you should wear

○ what questions you might be asked, both individually and as a team, and how you should prepare for them.

Once you've decided all this, carry out the tasks you've been allocated to the best of your ability and by the deadline agreed.

Organisation

This is about the planning you need to do as a team so that everything will run smoothly on the day.

Delivery

This refers to your performance during the presentation. Being well prepared and well organised helps you keep calm. If you're very nervous at the start, don't panic – just take a few deep breaths and concentrate on the task, not yourself. It's quite normal to be nervous at the start but this usually fades once you get under way. You might even enjoy it…

Case study: Ryan's presentation

Presenting information is a skill that takes time and experience to develop and get right.

Ryan doesn't like speaking in front of other people. He finds the process embarrassing and becomes very self-conscious. So how is he going to get through his presentation on fish management that is coming up shortly? He speaks to his tutor who gives him some advice.

"Ryan, remember to research your topic fully and keep your information simple and to the point. You're very knowledgeable on this subject so make sure you give the audience some of your own experiences.

"Your presentation doesn't need to be dry, add some humour where appropriate, and have some questions ready in case you suddenly find yourself forgetting what to say next. It's a good idea to practise to get your timing and content right."

Ryan finds this useful information. He takes his time to put together PowerPoint slides and is happy with the result. Ryan is now very nervous. His dad has watched a practice presentation and is impressed, but now it is time for the real thing. There are two presentations before his, which puts him more at ease. Everyone is supporting each other as everyone feels equally anxious.

During the presentation, Ryan only forgets what he is saying once but uses the questioning idea from his tutor, which helps out brilliantly. The positive feedback he receives reflects that the time he has spent preparing and rehearsing was used to good advantage. Ryan feels that next time he has to present something he will be less nervous and it will be much easier.

Activity: Practical solutions for presentations

Some common issues exist around having to make a presentation. Can you come up with some practical solutions to overcome them?

Issue	Solution
Nerves People often get a dry mouth, shake, stammer or forget what to say	
Technical problems IT systems fail, your presentation won't load, you forget how to use the equipment	
Bored faces People lose interest in what you are saying, you see yawning and fidgeting	
Intimidating audience People ask random questions they think you won't be able to answer or they are aggressive or rude	

Your assessments

The importance of assignments

All learners on BTEC First courses are assessed by means of **assignments**. Each one is designed to link to specific **learning outcomes** and **grading criteria**. At the end of the course, your assignment grades put together determine your overall grade.

To get the best grade you can, you need to know the golden rules that apply to all assignments, then how to interpret the specific instructions.

10 golden rules for assignments

1. Check that you understand the instructions.

2. Check whether you have to do all the work on your own, or if you will do some as a member of a group. If you work as a team, you need to identify which parts are your own contributions.

3. Always write down any verbal instructions you are given.

4. Check the final deadline and any penalties for not meeting it.

5. Make sure you know what to do if you have a serious personal problem, eg illness, and need an official extension.

6. Copying someone else's work (**plagiarism**) is a serious offence and is easy for experienced tutors to spot. It's never worth the risk.

7. Schedule enough time for finding out the information and doing initial planning.

8. Allow plenty of time between talking to your tutor about your plans, preparations and drafts, and the final deadline.

9. Don't panic if the assignment seems long or complicated. Break it down into small, manageable chunks.

10. If you suddenly get stuck, ask your tutor to talk things through with you.

Case study: Stacy receives feedback

Stacy receives feedback for her first assignment on animal health and wellbeing for her BTEC First in Animal Care. The feedback is clear and easy to follow.

"The assignment is a mixture of practical and theory tasks. It covered the P1, P2, M1 and D1 grading criteria for *Unit 4 Maintain Animal Health and Welfare.*

"For P1 we needed to demonstrate that we can recognise signs of normal and abnormal health in animals. Our tutor gave us worksheets and three different animals to check on over a period of time. The boxes on the worksheet are very detailed, but we were given a filled in one as an example. The P2 task linked with P1 as we had to carry out routine checks on animals, and this is covered on the same worksheet.

"For M1 we had to describe what to do when signs of abnormal health or ill health are found in specified animals during routine health checks. This has to be in a report-style paper.

I find this work fairly easy as it is really just reporting on the practical tasks we do.

"For D1, we had to describe possible causes and treatments for abnormal or ill health found in specified animals during routine health checks and include this in the same report as M1.

"I attempted all of the criteria for this assignment. I gained P1, P2 and M1. My tutor is happy that I aimed for a distinction, although I didn't manage to achieve it. Her feedback did clearly state why: *Well done Stacy, you have described possible causes of abnormal and ill health in the animals and included clearly labelled diagrams. However to gain a distinction grade you need to suggest possible treatments for the causes described.*

"I can see that my assignment brief asked for this, so I now know what I have to do to achieve a distinction".

Interpreting the instructions

Most assignments start with a **command word** – describe, explain, evaluate etc. These words relate to how complex the answer should be.

Command words

Learners often don't do their best because they read the command words but don't understand exactly what they have to do. These tables show you what is required for each grade when you see a particular command word.

Command words and obtaining a pass

Complete ...	Complete a form, diagram or drawing.
Demonstrate ...	Show that you can do a particular activity.
Describe ...	Give a clear, straightforward description that includes all the main points.
Identify ...	Give all the basic facts relating to a certain topic.
List ...	Write a list of the main items (not sentences).
Name ...	State the proper terms related to a drawing or diagram.
Outline ...	Give the main points, but without going into much detail.
State ...	Point out or list the main features.

Examples:

○ **List** the main features on your mobile phone.

○ **Describe** the best way to greet a customer.

○ **Outline** the procedures you follow to keep your computer system secure.

Command words and obtaining a merit

Analyse ...	Identify the factors that apply, and state how these are linked and how each of them relates to the topic.
Comment on ...	Give your own opinions or views.
Compare ... Contrast ...	Identify the main factors relating to two or more items and point out the similarities and differences.
Competently use ...	Take full account of information and feedback you have obtained to review or improve an activity.
Demonstrate ...	Prove you can carry out a more complex activity.
Describe ...	Give a full description, including details of all the relevant features.
Explain ...	Give logical reasons to support your views.
Justify ...	Give reasons for the points you are making so that the reader knows what you're thinking.
Suggest ...	Give your own ideas or thoughts.

Examples:
- **Explain** why mobile phones are so popular.
- **Describe** the needs of four different types of customers.
- **Suggest** the type of procedures your employer would need to introduce to keep the IT system secure.

Command words and obtaining a distinction

Analyse ...	Identify several relevant factors, show how they are linked, and explain the importance of each.
Compare ... Contrast ...	Identify the main factors in two or more situations, then explain the similarities and differences, and in some cases say which is best and why.
Demonstrate ...	Prove that you can carry out a complex activity, taking into account information you have obtained or received to adapt your original idea.
Describe ...	Give a comprehensive description which tells a story to the reader and shows that you can apply your knowledge and information correctly.
Evaluate ...	Bring together all your information and make a judgement on the importance or success of something.
Explain ...	Provide full details and reasons to support the arguments you are making.
Justify ...	Give full reasons or evidence to support your opinion.
Recommend ...	Weigh up all the evidence to come to a conclusion, with reasons, about what would be best.

Examples:
- **Evaluate** the features and performance of your mobile phone.
- **Analyse** the role of customer service in contributing to an organisation's success.
- **Justify** the main features on the website of a large, successful organisation of your choice.

TRY THIS

Check the command word you are likely to see for each of your units in the **grading grid** in advance. This tells you the **grading criteria** for the unit so that you know the evidence you will have to present.

TOP TIPS

Think of assignments as an opportunity to demonstrate what you've learned and to get feedback on your work.

Activity: Peer assessment and self-assessment

At times during your course you may be asked to assess the work of other learners on your course. This is known as peer assessment. Using the table below, state some of the advantages and disadvantages of using this method of assessment.

Peer assessment	
Advantages	**Disadvantages**

You may also be asked to self-assess your work. Use the table below, to show the advantages and disadvantages of using this method of assessment.

Self-assessment	
Advantages	**Disadvantages**

Sample assignment

Note about assignments
All learners are different and will approach their assignment in different ways.
The sample assignment that follows shows how one learner answered a brief to achieve pass, merit and distinction level criteria. The learner work shows just one way in which grading criteria can be evidenced. There are no standard or set answers. If you produce the required evidence for each task then you will achieve the grading criteria covered by the assignment.

Front sheet

Read the assignment front sheet through carefully and check your work links to the stated criteria.

Meeting deadlines is an essential part of your course. Make sure you find out your centre's policy on deadlines.

It is a good idea to go through your work with your tutor before submitting it, just in case you have misunderstood something.

If using someone else's work you must quote the source it came from both in your text and at the end of your work.

Learner name		Assessor name	
Ryan Connor		Miss Jade Ward	
Date issued	**Completion date**		**Submitted on**
4 October 2010	13 December 2010		6 December 2010
Qualification		**Unit**	
BTEC Level 2 Diploma in Countryside and Environment		Unit 5: Participate in Providing Estate Maintenance	

Assignment title	Being Safe and Considering the Environment

In this assignment you will have opportunities to provide evidence against the following criteria. Indicate the page numbers where the evidence can be found.

Criteria reference	To achieve the criteria the evidence must show that the student is able to:	Task no.	Evidence
P11	state the current environmental and health and safety legislation and codes of practice	1	1–4 and observation record
P12	describe how to overcome problems presented by services	2	5–6
P13	describe how environmental damage can be minimised	3	7–8
P14	describe how organic and inorganic waste may be disposed of	3	7–8

Learner declaration

I certify that the work submitted for this assignment is my own and research sources are fully acknowledged.

Learner signature: *Ryan Connor*   Date: *6 December 2010*

Ensure you are providing the specific evidence asked for and that it has been linked clearly to the criteria.

Assignment work should be your own and not copied from anyone else (this is plagiarism and it will not be accepted by your centre).

Assignment brief

An assignment scenario is designed to put the work into the context of land-based industries.

The assignment title will help you to plan your research.

Tutors may also need to provide evidence of your competence by signing observation sheets or witness statements.

Qualification	BTEC Level 2 Diploma in Countryside and Environment
Unit title	Unit 5: Participate in Providing Estate Maintenance
Start date	4 December 2010
Deadline date	13 December 2010
Assessor	Miss Jade Ward

Assignment title	Being Safe and Considering the Environment

The purpose of this assignment is to:
enable learners to gain the skills and understanding of health and safety and environmental legislations that will affect their practical work.

Scenario
You are working for a land-based business, and have been told that a school pupil is planning to work alongside you for their work experience. In the following tasks you will produce materials for them that explain the legislation that affects your work, how to overcome problems presented by services, and how to dispose of waste and minimise environmental damage.

Task 1
For this part of the assignment you will need to research current health and safety and environmental legislation and codes of practice within land-based industries and prepare a presentation which could be delivered to the school pupil and all others on work experience. This will be observed by your tutor and peers.

With your research materials, put together a presentation using a visual aid, eg slides, an overhead projector or a flip chart, which states the laws and legislations researched.

You must give a printed copy of this and your notes to your tutor.

Your tutor will provide an observation record to confirm your achievement.

This provides evidence for P11

Task 2
While working on an estate, services (eg Electricity, Water, Telephone) can cause problems. In a report style paper describe how to overcome problems presented by these services.

This provides evidence for P12

Task 3
Produce an informative leaflet that could be given to the school pupil on their work experience placement which includes the following information:
• How environmental damage can be minimised **(P13)**
• How organic and inorganic waste may be disposed of **(P14)**

This provides evidence for P13 and P14

Read tasks carefully to ensure you cover everything that has been asked of you.

Key words will be used throughout your assignments. Make sure you understand their meaning so you can meet the criteria, for example, here 'produce' means 'make'.

Use this list in your research. It will help ensure you draw on a range of sources. You will find some easier to access than others and you might want to ask your tutor for guidance on the best resources on the list.

Sources of information

Textbooks
Hessayon, D G – *Garden DIY Expert* (Expert, 1993) ISBN 9780903505376
Agate, E – *Toolcare: A Maintenance and Workshop Manual, Revised edition* (British Trust for Conservation Volunteers, 2000) ISBN 9780946752249
Sutherland, W J – *Managing Habitats for Conservation, 1st edition* (Cambridge University Press, 1995) ISBN 9780521447768

Leaflets
Health and Safety Executive leaflets, eg Manual Handling Assessment Charts (HSE, 2003)
The Environment Agency leaflets

Websites
Health and Safety Executive **www.hse.gov.uk**
The Environment Agency **www.environment-agency.gov.uk**
The Royal Horticultural Society **www.rhs.org.uk**
Department for environment, food and rural affairs **www.defra.gov.uk**

This brief has beeen verified as being fit for purpose			
Assessor	Miss Jade Ward		
Signature	Jade Ward	Date	20 September 2010
Internal verifier	Mr D Howard		
Signature	Dean Howard	Date	20 September 2010

Sample learner work

Copy of presentation slides included, as asked for in Task 1.

Current health and safety codes of practice given clearly.

Sample learner work: page 1

Task 1

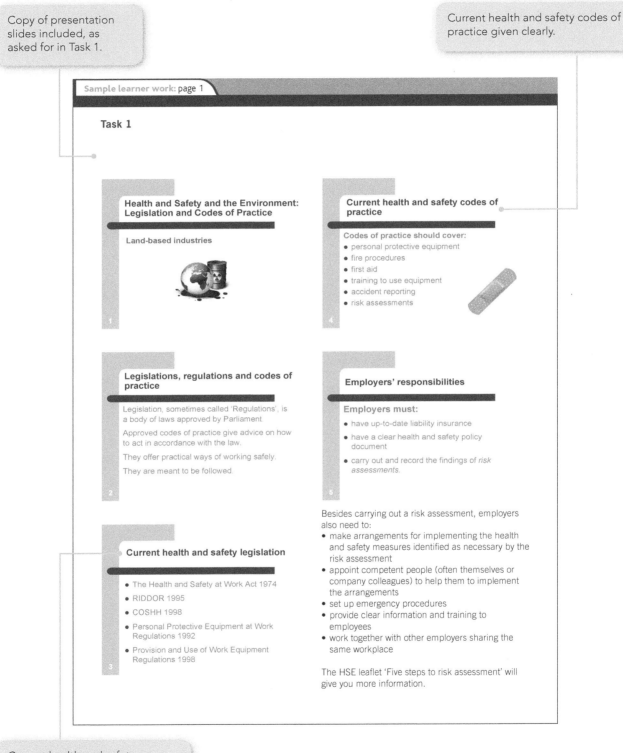

Health and Safety and the Environment: Legislation and Codes of Practice

Land-based industries

Legislations, regulations and codes of practice

Legislation, sometimes called 'Regulations', is a body of laws approved by Parliament.

Approved codes of practice give advice on how to act in accordance with the law.

They offer practical ways of working safely.

They are meant to be followed.

Current health and safety legislation

- The Health and Safety at Work Act 1974
- RIDDOR 1995
- COSHH 1998
- Personal Protective Equipment at Work Regulations 1992
- Provision and Use of Work Equipment Regulations 1998

Current health and safety codes of practice

Codes of practice should cover:
- personal protective equipment
- fire procedures
- first aid
- training to use equipment
- accident reporting
- risk assessments

Employers' responsibilities

Employers must:
- have up-to-date liability insurance
- have a clear health and safety policy document
- carry out and record the findings of *risk assessments*.

Besides carrying out a risk assessment, employers also need to:
- make arrangements for implementing the health and safety measures identified as necessary by the risk assessment
- appoint competent people (often themselves or company colleagues) to help them to implement the arrangements
- set up emergency procedures
- provide clear information and training to employees
- work together with other employers sharing the same workplace

The HSE leaflet 'Five steps to risk assessment' will give you more information.

Current health and safety legislation set out clearly. It is excellent practice to include the dates of the legislation.

Current environmental legislation and codes of practice are clearly stated.

Slides 9–13 show clear research of the current health and safety legislation and codes of practice as asked for.

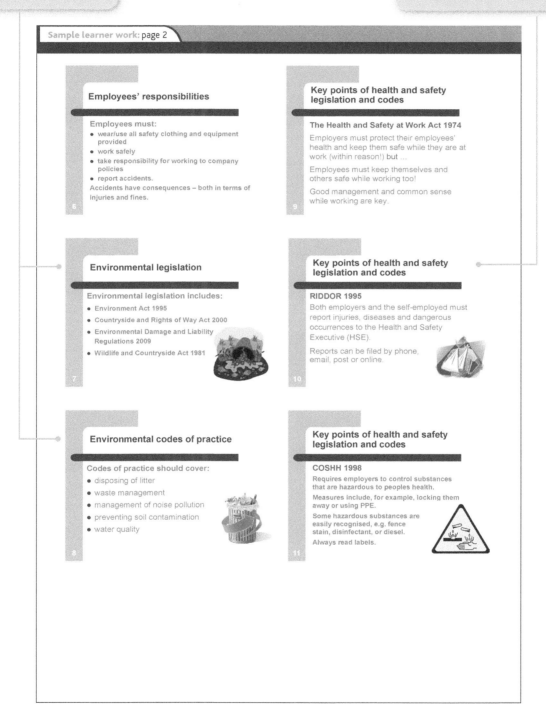

Sample learner work: page 2

Employees' responsibilities

Employees must:
- wear/use all safety clothing and equipment provided
- work safely
- take responsibility for working to company policies
- report accidents.

Accidents have consequences – both in terms of injuries and fines.

6

Environmental legislation

Environmental legislation includes:
- Environment Act 1995
- Countryside and Rights of Way Act 2000
- Environmental Damage and Liability Regulations 2009
- Wildlife and Countryside Act 1981

7

Environmental codes of practice

Codes of practice should cover:
- disposing of litter
- waste management
- management of noise pollution
- preventing soil contamination
- water quality

8

Key points of health and safety legislation and codes

The Health and Safety at Work Act 1974

Employers must protect their employees' health and keep them safe while they are at work (within reason!) but ...

Employees must keep themselves and others safe while working too!

Good management and common sense while working are key.

9

Key points of health and safety legislation and codes

RIDDOR 1995

Both employers and the self-employed must report injuries, diseases and dangerous occurrences to the Health and Safety Executive (HSE).

Reports can be filed by phone, email, post or online.

10

Key points of health and safety legislation and codes

COSHH 1998

Requires employers to control substances that are hazardous to peoples health.

Measures include, for example, locking them away or using PPE.

Some hazardous substances are easily recognised, e.g. fence stain, disinfectant, or diesel.

Always read labels.

11

Slides 14–17 show good research on the current environmental legislation and codes of practice as asked for in the task outline in the assignment brief.

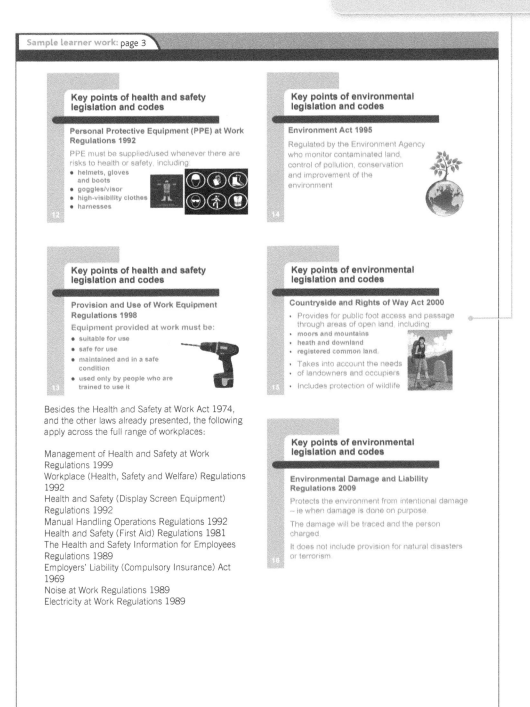

Key points of health and safety legislation and codes

Personal Protective Equipment (PPE) at Work Regulations 1992

PPE must be supplied/used whenever there are risks to health or safety, including:

- helmets, gloves and boots
- goggles/visor
- high-visibility clothes
- harnesses

Key points of health and safety legislation and codes

Provision and Use of Work Equipment Regulations 1998

Equipment provided at work must be:

- suitable for use
- safe for use
- maintained and in a safe condition
- used only by people who are trained to use it

Key points of environmental legislation and codes

Environment Act 1995

Regulated by the Environment Agency who monitor contaminated land, control of pollution, conservation and improvement of the environment

Key points of environmental legislation and codes

Countryside and Rights of Way Act 2000

- Provides for public foot access and passage through areas of open land, including:
  - moors and mountains
  - heath and downland
  - registered common land.
- Takes into account the needs of landowners and occupiers
- Includes protection of wildlife

Key points of environmental legislation and codes

Environmental Damage and Liability Regulations 2009

Protects the environment from intentional damage – ie when damage is done on purpose.

The damage will be traced and the person charged.

It does not include provision for natural disasters or terrorism.

Besides the Health and Safety at Work Act 1974, and the other laws already presented, the following apply across the full range of workplaces:

Management of Health and Safety at Work Regulations 1999
Workplace (Health, Safety and Welfare) Regulations 1992
Health and Safety (Display Screen Equipment) Regulations 1992
Manual Handling Operations Regulations 1992
Health and Safety (First Aid) Regulations 1981
The Health and Safety Information for Employees Regulations 1989
Employers' Liability (Compulsory Insurance) Act 1969
Noise at Work Regulations 1989
Electricity at Work Regulations 1989

The learner's bibliography shows research undertaken for the task.

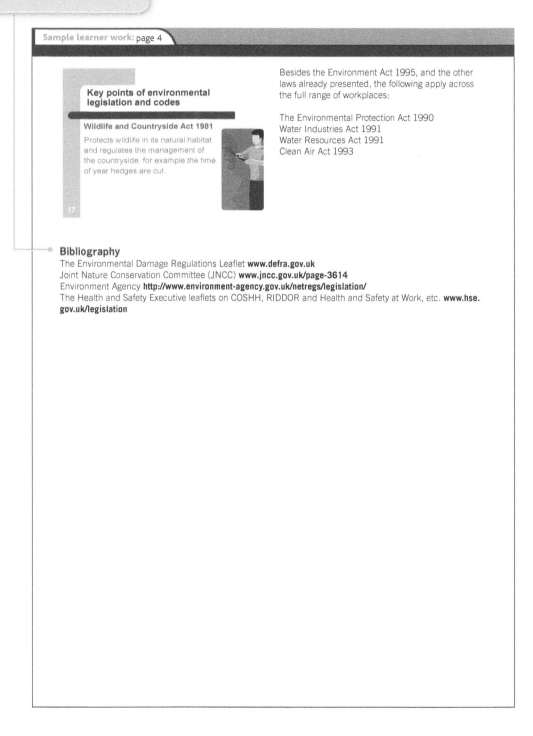

Sample learner work: page 4

Key points of environmental legislation and codes

Wildlife and Countryside Act 1981

Protects wildlife in its natural habitat and regulates the management of the countryside, for example the time of year hedges are cut.

Besides the Environment Act 1995, and the other laws already presented, the following apply across the full range of workplaces:

The Environmental Protection Act 1990
Water Industries Act 1991
Water Resources Act 1991
Clean Air Act 1993

Bibliography
The Environmental Damage Regulations Leaflet **www.defra.gov.uk**
Joint Nature Conservation Committee (JNCC) **www.jncc.gov.uk/page-3614**
Environment Agency **http://www.environment-agency.gov.uk/netregs/legislation/**
The Health and Safety Executive leaflets on COSHH, RIDDOR and Health and Safety at Work, etc. **www.hse.gov.uk/legislation**

Competence in carrying out a practical activity is confirmed by your tutor completing an observation record.

Observation record for Task 1

Learner name	Ryan Connor
Programme	BTEC Level 2 First Diploma in Countryside and Environment
Unit number and title	Unit 5: Participate in Providing Estate Maintenance
Assignment title	Being Safe and Considering the Environment

Description of activity undertaken (please be as specific as possible)

Task 1:
Slide presentation to the class on current health and safety and environmental legislation and codes of practice within land-based industries

Assessment and grading criteria

P11
State the current environmental and health and safety legislation and codes of practice

How the activity meets the requirements of the assessment and grading criteria

A clear presentation which stated current health and safety and environmental legislation and codes of practice within land-based industries. The slides were very clear and well laid out. Ryan slightly rushed through the beginning but otherwise kept a clear tone, made good eye contact and only read from notes when needed. Notes handed in, **P11 Met**.

Assessor signature	Jade Ward		Date	25 October 2010
Assessor name	Miss Jade Ward			

Always check your tutor has signed this document for you.

A well presented report which has clear headings and links to the criterion.

It is good practice to highlight which criterion work links to.

Task 2: Services Report on the College Estate (P12)

Introduction
In this report I will be describing how you can overcome problems that are presented by services on an estate as well as investigating the authorities that are responsible for supplying these services. I will also be naming alternative suppliers for these services. The estate I will be investigating will be the college grounds which we use for this assignment.

My Estate
The college grounds are about 30 acres which are made up of several areas. There are mature gardens, buildings for teaching, a reception building, learner accommodation, four glasshouses and fields.

How to overcome problems presented by services:
Water
The mains water with a water meter comes from the road at the front of the college; it then flows through the site to all the water points. There are five outside taps placed around the gardens for watering in the summer months. The problem with this service is that we cannot dig anywhere near these taps because the pipe is underground. The taps are hidden from view within the garden areas and it is easy to forget where they are. A way round this would be a map drawn up with the water pipes highlighted on it so that everyone knew where they were. Another problem is that in the winter months the pipes freeze. The pipes are old and can suffer with cracks and split. A way round this is to use lagging so they are protected and to check on them regularly. If an outside tap isn't checked and it splits, the damage could cost a lot of money to repair.

Suppliers
The water on my estate is supplied by:
  Anglian Water
  PO Box 770
  Lincoln
  LN5 7WX

An alternative supplier of this service could be:
  Cambridge Water
  41 Rustat Road
  Cambridge
  CB1 3QS

However Cambridge Water can only supply water, they cannot take it away. Waste water is only dealt with by Anglian Water.

Electricity
The electricity on my estate is supplied by overhead cables; this comes in via the bottom of our site. Most of the electricity is well away from any working areas except from one line that comes into the teaching building. There are several trees around this area that need regular pruning. This is a dangerous job. This problem could be overcome safely by using a contractor to prune these trees using the correct equipment. Properly trained contractors would come in with a cherry picker and chainsaws to undertake this task.

Suppliers
The electricity on my estate is supplied by:
  EDF Energy
  Osprey House
  Osprey Road
  EXETER
  EX2 7WN

An alternative supplier of this service could be British Gas (Electric) **0800 048 0202**

Information given is factual and to the point.

Pictures used by the learner adds interest to the report. Using company logos here would have been a nice touch.

Pictures used by the learner adds interest to the report. Using company logos here would have been a nice touch.

Sample learner work: page 6

Gas

The gas on the estate is not via mains but is supplied through Calor Gas cylinders. Gas is used for the glasshouse heating and has caused problems in the past. Firstly during a very cold period they ran out because all the staff were away on holiday over the Christmas period, so some plants ended up dying. This meant that our estate lost lots of money. A way round this would be to always have a back up of spare supplies, or two cylinders connected so we would know when one was empty. Also having staff on a rota would mean that someone could check on them everyday. Another problem that needs to be overcome is theft. Several bottles of gas have been stolen as they are kept outside. A way round this would be to lock them up in a purpose built shed or to move them inside the glasshouse but make sure they were hidden.

Suppliers

The calor gas bottles are supplied by:
LPG Gas Supply Ltd
Wisbech
Cambridgeshire

An alternative supplier could be:
Calor Gas Limited
Athena House
Athena Drive
Tachbrook Park
Warwick CV34 6RL

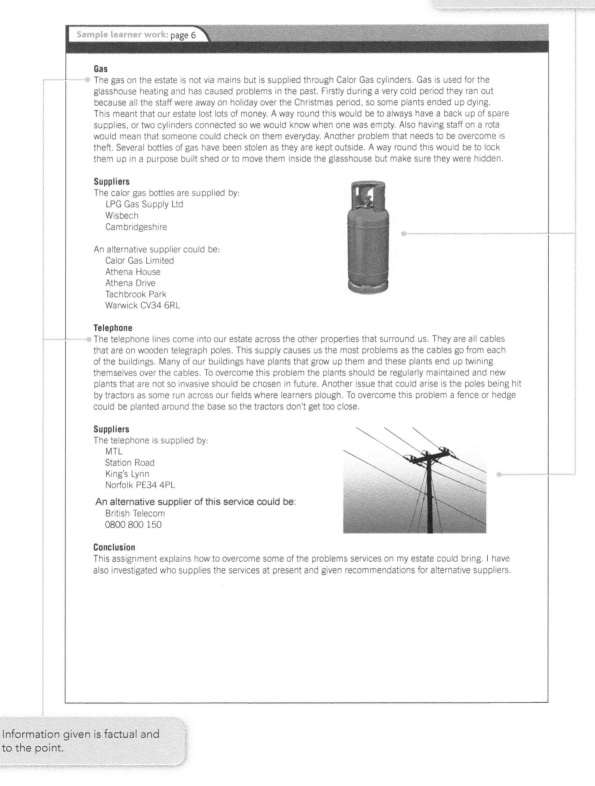

Telephone

The telephone lines come into our estate across the other properties that surround us. They are all cables that are on wooden telegraph poles. This supply causes us the most problems as the cables go from each of the buildings. Many of our buildings have plants that grow up them and these plants end up twining themselves over the cables. To overcome this problem the plants should be regularly maintained and new plants that are not so invasive should be chosen in future. Another issue that could arise is the poles being hit by tractors as some run across our fields where learners plough. To overcome this problem a fence or hedge could be planted around the base so the tractors don't get too close.

Suppliers

The telephone is supplied by:
MTL
Station Road
King's Lynn
Norfolk PE34 4PL

An alternative supplier of this service could be:
British Telecom
0800 800 150

Conclusion

This assignment explains how to overcome some of the problems services on my estate could bring. I have also investigated who supplies the services at present and given recommendations for alternative suppliers.

Information given is factual and to the point.

Sample learner work: page 7

Task 3: 'How to minimise environmental damage' leaflet (P13 and P14)

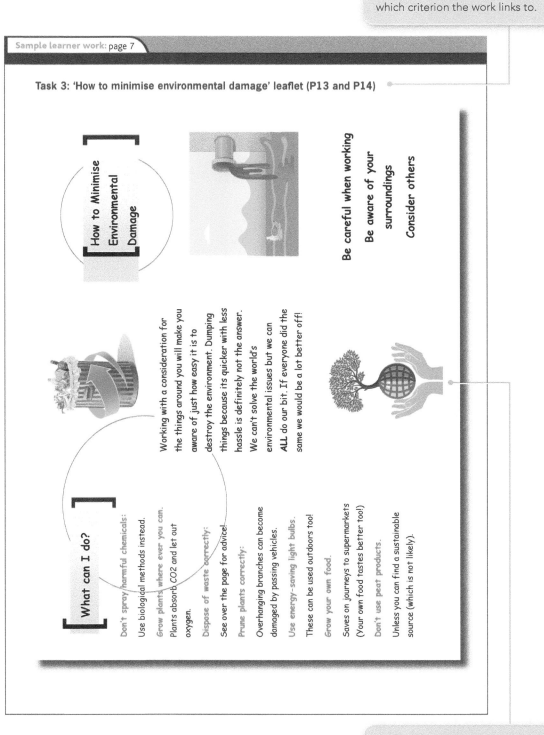

How to Minimise Environmental Damage

Be careful when working
Be aware of your surroundings
Consider others

What can I do?

Working with a consideration for the things around you will make you aware of just how easy it is to destroy the environment. Dumping things because its quicker with less hassle is definitely not the answer. We can't solve the world's environmental issues but we can ALL do our bit. If everyone did the same we would be a lot better off!

Don't spray harmful chemicals:
Use biological methods instead.

Grow plants where ever you can.
Plants absorb CO2 and let out oxygen.

Dispose of waste correctly:
See over the page for advice!

Prune plants correctly:
Overhanging branches can become damaged by passing vehicles.

Use energy-saving light bulbs.
These can be used outdoors too!

Grow your own food.
Saves on journeys to supermarkets (Your own food tastes better too!)

Don't use peat products.
Unless you can find a sustainable source (which is not likely).

Learner's information is clear, to the point, easy to read and links to the criterion.

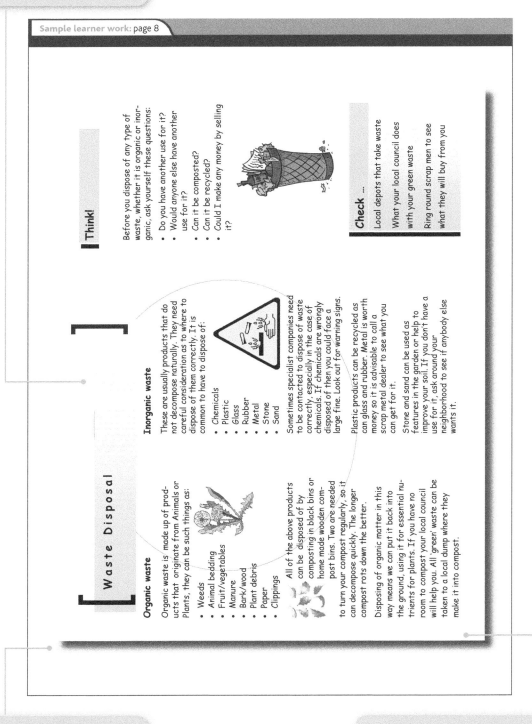

Waste Disposal

Organic waste

Organic waste is made up of products that originate from Animals or Plants, they can be such things as:

- Weeds
- Animal bedding
- Fruit/vegetables
- Manure
- Bark/wood
- Plant debris
- Paper
- Clippings

All of the above products can be disposed of by composting in black bins or home made wooden compost bins. Two are needed to turn your compost regularly, so it can decompose quickly. The longer compost rots down the better.

Disposing of organic matter in this way means we can put it back into the ground, using it for essential nutrients for plants. If you have no room to compost your local council will help you. All 'green' waste can be taken to a local dump where they make it into compost.

Inorganic waste

These are usually products that do not decompose naturally. They need careful consideration as to where to dispose of them correctly. It is common to have to dispose of:

- Chemicals
- Plastic
- Glass
- Rubber
- Metal
- Stone
- Sand

Sometimes specialist companies need to be contacted to dispose of waste correctly, especially in the case of chemicals. If chemicals are wrongly disposed of then you could face a large fine. Look out for warning signs.

Plastic products can be recycled as can glass and rubber. Metal is worth money so it is advisable to call a scrap metal dealer to see what you can get for it.

Stone and sand can be used as features in the garden or help to improve your soil. If you don't have a use for it, ask around your neighborhood to see if anybody else wants it.

Think!

Before you dispose of any type of waste, whether it is organic or inorganic, ask yourself these questions:

- Do you have another use for it?
- Would anyone else have another use for it?
- Can it be composted?
- Can it be recycled?
- Could I make any money by selling it?

Check ...

- Local depots that take waste
- What your local council does with your green waste
- Ring round scrap men to see what they will buy from you

Remember: when making something like a leaflet or poster look at other examples in your industry area for ideas.

A bibliography should have been included at the end of this assignment to list the sources used when researching material for the report and the leaflet.

Assessor's comments

This feedback will give your tutor an idea of how you feel about the assignment. Being honest will help your own learning and could help future learners if any areas of the assignment could be improved or simplified.

A yes will indicate that you have achieved the criteria. If a no is given, clear guidance will be provided on why you did not achieve the criterion and what you need to do to improve your work.

Qualification	BTEC Level 2 First Diploma in Countryside and Environment	Year	2010–2011
Unit number and title	Unit 5: Participate in Providing Estate Maintenance	Learner name	Ryan Connor
Assignment title	Being Safe and Considering the Environment		

Grading criteria	Achieved?
P11 state the current environmental and health and safety legislation and codes of practice	Yes
P12 describe how to overcome problems presented by services	Yes
P13 describe how environmental damage can be minimised	Yes
P14 describe how organic and inorganic waste may be disposed of	Yes

Learner feedback

I really liked doing this assignment as it had lots of different tasks to do which I enjoyed. I especially liked the presentation as it was much easier than just writing about something. I also liked making a leaflet on the computer. I have never done that before and I could make it look quite professional.

Assessor feedback

This is an excellent assignment Ryan with some very interesting points. Your work is informative, well presented and meets all the criteria asked for. Well done on this standard of work, keep it up!

Action plan

It is important to give details of your research in a bibliography or reference page for each task.

| Assessor signature | Jade Ward | | Date | 13 December 2010 |
| Learner signature | Ryan Connor | | Date | 20 December 2010 |

Always read your tutor's feedback. This one is very positive, which helps motivate future learning. Often guidance will be given here which will detail improvements or ways to achieve higher grades.

Action plans also give clear guidance and dates to ensure you know what improvements to make and by when.

An action plan will state what else may be needed to complete an assignment. An assignment could have passed but actions for improvement are still given to help with future work.

Coping with problems

Most learners sail through their BTEC First with no major problems. Unfortunately, not everyone is so lucky. Some may have personal difficulties or other issues that disrupt their work so they are late handing in their assignments. If this happens to you, it's vital to know what to do. This checklist should help.

TOP TIPS

If you have a serious complaint or concern, talk to your chosen tutor first – for example if you believe an assignment grade is unfair. All centres have official procedures to cover important issues such as appeals about assignments and formal complaints, but it's sensible to try to resolve a problem informally first.

Checklist for coping with problems

✔ Check that you know who to talk to.

✔ Don't sit on a problem and worry about it. Talk to someone promptly, in confidence. It's always easier to cope if you've shared it with someone.

✔ Most centres have professional counsellors you can talk to if you prefer. They won't repeat anything you say to them without your permission.

✔ If you've done something wrong or silly, people will respect you more if you are honest, admit where you went wrong and apologise promptly.

Case study: Speak up, someone can help you

Sophia lost her part-time job recently. She has been using her wages to get a bus pass to get to college and to pay for the equipment she needs to do her course. She hasn't told anyone as things are tight at home and she doesn't want her parents to worry. She thinks she can figure things out.

Unfortunately, Sophia's college attendance becomes erratic. She misses days and often arrives late. Her work is starting to suffer and she gets in trouble for not bringing equipment to practical classes.

Sophia's course tutor calls her in for a one-to-one tutorial to discuss her poor attendance. At first, Sophia brushes off her poor attendance as being unwell. However, after a while, Sophia realises it is time to come clean.

She explains about losing her job and, because she has no money for a bus pass, having to walk which makes her late. She also explains that she sold her personal protective equipment to pay for lunch, and doesn't want her parents to know in case they might worry.

Sophia's tutor suggests they pay a visit to the student support staff together for advice. She soon finds out that she could be eligible for Educational Maintenance Allowance (EMA) payments of £30 per week. She may also be able to access a grant to pay for her equipment. Sophia's tutor calls in her parents to help complete the forms and get the processes underway.

"I'm very relieved to talk to someone about my problems. I had no idea I could get EMA and help with my equipment. I came very close to losing my college place as I got quite behind with my work. Lucky for me my friends and tutor are helping me to catch up."

Skills building

To do your best in your assignments you need a number of skills, including:
- your **personal, learning and thinking skills**
- your **functional skills** of ICT, mathematics and English
- your proofreading and document-production skills.

Personal, learning and thinking skills (PLTS)

These are the skills, personal qualities and behaviour that you find in people who are effective and confident at work. These people enjoy carrying out a wide range of tasks, always try to do their best, and work well alone or with others. They enjoy a challenge and use new experiences to learn and develop.

Activity: How good are your PLTS?

1 Do this quiz to help you identify areas for improvement.

a) I get on well with other people.

Always   **Usually**   **Seldom**   **Never**

b) I try to find out other people's suggestions for solving problems that puzzle me.

Always   **Usually**   **Seldom**   **Never**

c) I plan carefully to make sure I meet my deadlines.

Always   **Usually**   **Seldom**   **Never**

d) If someone is being difficult, I think carefully before making a response.

Always   **Usually**   **Seldom**   **Never**

e) I don't mind sharing my possessions or my time.

Always   **Usually**   **Seldom**   **Never**

f) I take account of other people's views and opinions.

Always   **Usually**   **Seldom**   **Never**

g) I enjoy thinking of new ways of doing things.

Always   **Usually**   **Seldom**   **Never**

h) I like creating new and different things.

Always   **Usually**   **Seldom**   **Never**

i) I enjoy planning and finding ways of solving problems.

Always   **Usually**   **Seldom**   **Never**

j) I enjoy getting feedback about my performance.

Always   Usually   Seldom   Never

k) I try to learn from constructive criticism so that I know what to improve.

Always   Usually   Seldom   Never

l) I enjoy new challenges.

Always   Usually   Seldom   Never

m) I am even-tempered.

Always   Usually   Seldom   Never

n) I am happy to make changes when necessary.

Always   Usually   Seldom   Never

o) I like helping other people.

Always   Usually   Seldom   Never

Score 3 points for each time you answered 'Always', 2 points for 'Usually', 1 point for 'Seldom' and 0 points for 'Never'. The higher your score, the higher your personal, learning and thinking skills.

2 How creative are you? Test yourself with this activity. Identify 50 different objects you could fit into a matchbox at the same time! As a start, three suitable items are a postage stamp, a grain of rice, a staple. Can you find 47 more?

BTEC FACTS

Your BTEC First qualification is at Level 2. Qualifications in functional skills start at Entry level and continue to Level 2. (You don't need to achieve functional skills to gain any BTEC qualification, and the evidence from a BTEC assignment can't be used towards the assessment of functional skills.)

Functional skills

Functional skills are the practical skills you need to function confidently, effectively and independently at work, when studying and in everyday life. They focus on the following areas:

- Information and Communications Technology (ICT)
- Maths
- English.

You may already be familiar with functional skills. Your BTEC First tutors will give you more information about how you will continue to develop these skills on your new course.

ICT skills

These will relate directly to how much 'hands-on' practice you have had on IT equipment. You may be an experienced IT user, and using word-processing, spreadsheet and presentation software may be second nature. Searching for information online may be something you do every day – in between downloading music, buying or selling on eBay and updating your Facebook profile!

Or you may prefer to avoid computer contact as much as possible. If so, there are two things you need to do.

1 Use every opportunity to improve your ICT skills so that you can start to live in the 21st century!

2 Make life easier by improving your basic proofreading and document preparation skills.

Proofreading and document preparation skills

Being able to produce well-displayed work quickly will make your life a lot easier. On any course there will be at least one unit that requires you to use good document preparation skills.

Tips to improve your document production skills

✔ If your keyboarding skills are poor, ask if there is a workshop you can join. Or your library or resource centre may have software you can use.

✔ Check that you know the format of documents you have to produce for assignments. It can help to have a 'model' version of each type in your folder for quick reference.

✔ Practise checking your work by reading word by word – and remember not to rely on spellcheckers (see page 56).

Activity: How good are your ICT skills?

1a) Test your current ICT abilities by responding *honestly* to each of the following statements.

i) I can create a copy of my timetable using a word-processing or spreadsheet package.
True   **False**

ii) I can devise and design a budget for myself for the next three months using a spreadsheet package.
True   **False**

iii) I can email a friend who has just got broadband to say how to minimise the danger of computer viruses, what a podcast is, and also explain the restrictions on music downloads.
True   **False**

iv) I can use presentation software to prepare a presentation containing four or five slides on a topic of my choice.
True   **False**

v) I can research online to compare the performance and prices of laptop computers and prepare an information sheet using word-processing software.
True   **False**

vi) I can prepare a poster, with graphics, for my mother's friend, who is starting her own business preparing children's party food, and attach it to an email to her for approval.
True   **False**

TRY THIS

Learning to touch-type can save you hours of time. Go to page 90 to find out how to access a website where you can check your keyboarding skills.

TOP TIPS

Print your work on good paper and keep it flat so that it looks good when you hand it in.

1b) Select any one of the above to which you answered false and learn how to do it.

2 Compare the two tables below. The first is an original document; the second is a typed copy. Are they identical? Highlight any differences you find and check them with the key on page 89.

Name	Date	Time	Room
Abbott	16 July	9.30 am	214
Grey	10 August	10.15 am	160
Johnston	12 August	2.20 pm	208
Waverley	18 July	3.15 pm	180
Jackson	30 September	11.15 am	209
Gregory	31 August	4.20 pm	320
Marshall	10 September	9.30 am	170
Bradley	16 September	2.20 pm	210

Name	Date	Time	Room
Abbott	26 July	9.30 am	214
Gray	10 August	10.15 am	160
Johnson	12 August	2.20 pm	208
Waverley	18 July	3.15 am	180
Jackson	31 September	11.15 am	209
Gregory	31 August	4.20 pm	320
Marshall	10 September	9.30 pm	170
Bradley	16 August	2.20 pm	201

Maths or numeracy skills

Four easy ways to improve your numeracy skills

1 Work out simple calculations in your head, like adding up the prices of items you are buying. Then check if you are correct when you pay for them.

2 Set yourself numeracy problems based on your everyday life. For example, if you are on a journey that takes 35 minutes and you leave home at 11.10am, what time will you arrive? If you are travelling at 40 miles an hour, how long will it take you to go 10 miles?

3 Treat yourself to a Maths Training program.

4 Check out online sites to improve your skills. Go to page 90 to find out how to access a useful BBC website.

TOP TIPS

Quickly test answers. For example, if fuel costs 85p a litre and someone is buying 15 litres, estimate this at £1 x 15 (£15) and the answer should be just below this. So if your answer came out at £140, you'd immediately know you'd done something wrong!

Activity: How good are your maths skills?

Answer as many of the following questions as you can in 15 minutes. Check your answers with the key on page 89.

1 **a)** 12 + 28 = ?

   i) 30   ii) 34   iii) 38   iv) 40   v) 48

   b) 49 ÷ 7 = ?

   i) 6   ii) 7   iii) 8   iv) 9   v) 10

   c) ½ + 1¼ = ?

   i) ¾   ii) 1½   iii) 1¾   iv) 2¼   v) 3

   d) 4 × 12 = 8 × ?

   i) 5   ii) 6   iii) 7   iv) 8   v) 9

   e) 16.5 + 25.25 – ? = 13.25

   i) 28.5   ii) 31.25 iii) 34.5 iv) 41.65 v) 44

2 **a)** You buy four items at £1.99, two at 98p and three at £1.75. You hand over a £20 note. How much change will you get? _____

   b) What fraction of one litre is 250 ml? _____

   c) What percentage of £50 is £2.50? _____

   d) A designer travelling on business can claim 38.2p a mile in expenses. How much is she owed if she travels 625 miles? _____

   e) You are flying to New York in December. New York is five hours behind British time and the flight lasts eight hours. If you leave at 11.15 am, what time will you arrive? _____

   f) For your trip to the United States you need American dollars. You find that the exchange rate is $1.5 dollars.

   i)   How many dollars will you receive if you exchange £500? _____

   ii) Last year your friend visited New York when the exchange rate was $1.8. She also exchanged £500. Did she receive more dollars than you or fewer – and by how much? _____

   g) A security guard and his dog patrol the perimeter fence of a warehouse each evening. The building is 480 metres long and 300 metres wide and the fence is 80 metres out from the building on all sides. If the guard and his dog patrol the fence three times a night, how far will they walk? _____

English skills

Your English skills affect your ability to understand what you read, prepare a written document, say what you mean and understand other people. Even if you're doing a practical subject, there will always be times when you need to leave someone a note, tell them about a phone call, read or listen to instructions – or write a letter for a job application!

BTEC FACTS

Reading, writing, speaking and listening are all part of the Functional English qualifications.

TOP TIPS

If someone you're talking to uses a word, phrase or abbreviation you don't know, ask them what it means.

Six easy ways to improve your English skills

1 Read more. It increases the number of words you know and helps to make you familiar with correct spellings.

2 Look up words you don't understand in a dictionary and check their meaning. Then try to use them yourself to increase your vocabulary.

3 Do crosswords. These help increase your vocabulary and practise your spelling at the same time.

4 You can use websites to help you get to grips with English vocabulary, grammar and punctuation. Go to page 90 to find out how to access a useful BBC website.

5 Welcome opportunities to practise speaking in class, in discussion groups and during presentations – rather than avoiding them!

6 Test your ability to listen to someone else by seeing how much you can remember when they've finished speaking.

Activity: How good are your English skills?

1 In the table below are 'wrong' versions of words often spelled incorrectly. Write the correct spellings on the right. Check your list against the answers on page 89.

Incorrect spelling	Correct spelling
accomodation	
seperate	
definate	
payed	
desparate	
acceptible	
competant	
succesful	

2 Correct the error(s) in these sentences.

a) The plug on the computer is lose.

b) The car was stationery outside the house.

c) Their going on they're holidays tomorrow.

d) The principle of the college is John Smith.

e) We are all going accept Tom.

3 Punctuate these sentences correctly.

a) Toms train was late on Monday and Tuesday.

b) She is going to France Belgium Spain and Italy in the summer.

c) He comes from Leeds and says its great there.

4 Read the article on copyright.

Copyright

Anyone who uses a photocopier can break copyright law if they carry out unrestricted photocopying of certain documents. This is because The Copyright, Designs and Patents Act 1988 protects the creator of an original work against having it copied without permission.

Legally, every time anyone writes a book, composes a song, makes a film or creates any other type of artistic work, this work is treated as their property (or copyright). If anyone else wishes to make use of it, they must get permission to do so and, on occasions, pay a fee.

Licences can be obtained to allow educational establishments to photocopy limited numbers of some publications. In addition, copies of an original document can be made for certain specific purposes. These include research and private study. Under the Act, too, if an article is summarised and quoted by anyone, then the author and title of the original work must be acknowledged.

a) Test your ability to understand unfamiliar information by responding to the following statements with 'True' or 'False'.

i) Students and tutors in schools and colleges can copy anything they want.
True   False

ii) The law which covers copyright is The Copyright, Designs and Patents Act 1988.
True   False

iii) A student photocopying a document in the library must have a licence.
True   False

iv) Copyright only relates to books in the library.
True   False

v) If you quote a newspaper report in an assignment, you don't need to state the source.
True   False

vii) Anyone is allowed to photocopy a page of a book for research purposes.
True   False

b) Make a list of key points in the article, then write a brief summary in your own words.

5 Nikki has read a newspaper report that a horse racing in the Kentucky Derby had to be put down. The filly collapsed and the vet couldn't save her. Nikki says it's the third time in two years a racehorse has had to be put down in the US. As a horse lover she is convinced racing should be banned in Britain and the US. She argues that fox hunting was banned to protect foxes, and that racehorses are more important and more expensive than foxes. Darren disagrees. He says the law is not working, hardly anyone has been prosecuted and fox hunting is going on just like before. Debbie says that animals aren't important whilst there is famine in the world.

a) Do you think the three arguments are logical? See if you can spot the flaws and check your ideas with the suggestions on page 89.

b) Sporting activities and support for sporting teams often provoke strong opinions. For a sport or team of your choice, identify two opposing views that might be held. Then decide how you would give a balanced view. Test your ideas with a friend or family member.

Answers

Skills building answers

ICT activities

2 Differences between the two tables are highlighted in bold.

Name	Date	Time	Room
Abbott	**16** July	9.30 am	214
Grey	10 August	10.15 am	160
Johnston	12 August	2.20 pm	208
Waverley	18 July	3.15 **pm**	180
Jackson	**30** September	11.15 am	209
Gregory	31 August	4.20 pm	320
Marshall	10 September	9.30 **am**	170
Bradley	16 **September**	2.20 pm	**210**

Maths/numeracy activities

1 **a)** iv, **b)** ii, **c)** iii, **d)** ii, **e)** i
2 **a)** £4.83, **b)** ¼, **c)** 5%, **d)** £238.75, **e)** 2.15 pm, **f) i)** $750 **ii)** $150 dollars more, **g)** 6.6 km.

English activities

1 Spellings: accommodation, separate, definite, paid, desperate, acceptable, competent, successful

2 Errors:
   a) The plug on the computer is <u>loose</u>.
   b) The car was <u>stationary</u> outside the house.
   c) <u>They're</u> going on <u>their</u> holidays tomorrow.
   d) The <u>principal</u> of the college is John Smith.
   e) We are all going <u>except</u> Tom.

3 Punctuation:
   a) Tom's train was late on Monday and Tuesday.
   b) She is going to France, Belgium, Spain and Italy in the summer.
   c) He comes from Leeds and says it's great there.

4 **a) i)** False, **ii)** True, **iii)** False, **iv)** False, **v)** False, **vi)** False, **vii)** True

5 A logical argument would be that if racehorses are frequently injured in a particular race, eg one with difficult jumps, then it should not be held. It is not logical to compare racehorses with foxes. The value of the animal is irrelevant if you are assessing cruelty. Darren's argument is entirely different and unrelated to Nikki's. Whether or not fox hunting legislation is effective or not has no bearing on the danger (or otherwise) to racehorses. Finally, famine is a separate issue altogether. You cannot logically 'rank' problems in the world to find a top one and ignore the others until this is solved!

Accessing website links

Links to various websites are referred to throughout this BTEC Level 2 First Study Skills Guide. In order to ensure that there links are up-to-date, that they work and that the sites aren't inadvertently linked to any material that could be considered offensive, we have made links available on our website: www.pearsonhotlinks.co.uk. When you visit the site, please enter the title BTEC Level 2 First Study Skills Guide in Land and Environment or the ISBN 9781846909252 to gain access to the website links and information on how they can be used to help you with your studies.

Useful terms

Apprenticeships
Schemes that enable you to work and earn money at the same time as you gain further qualifications (an NVQ award and a technical certificate) and improve your functional skills. Apprentices learn work-based skills relevant to their job role and their chosen industry.Go to page 90 to find out how to access useful websites.

Assessment methods
Methods, such as practical tasks and assignments, which are used to check that your work demonstrates the learning and understanding you need to obtain the qualification.

Assessor
The tutor who marks or assesses your work.

Assignment
A complete task or mini-**project** set to meet specific grading criteria.

Assignment brief
The information and instructions related to a particular assignment.

BTEC Level 3 Nationals
Qualifications you can take when you have successfully achieved a Level 2 qualification, such as BTEC First. They are offered in a variety of subjects.

Credit value
The number of credits attached to your BTEC course. The credit value increases relative to the length of time you need to complete the course, from 15 credits for a BTEC Certificate, to 30 credits for a BTEC Extended Certificate and 60 credits for a BTEC Diploma.

Command word
The word in an assignment that tells you what you have to do to produce the type of answer that is required, eg 'list', 'describe', 'analyse'.

Educational Maintenance Award (EMA)
This is a means-tested award which provides eligible learners under 19 who are studying a full-time course at a centre with a cash sum of money every week. Go to page 90 to find out how to access useful websites.

Functional skills
The practical skills that enable all learners to use and apply English, Maths and ICT both at work and in their everyday lives. They aren't compulsory to achieve on the course, but are of great use to you.

Grade
The rating of pass, merit or distinction that is given to an assignment you have completed, which identifies the standard you have achieved.

Grading criteria
The standard you have to demonstrate to obtain a particular grade in the unit. In other words, what you have to prove you can do.

Grading grid
The table in each unit of your BTEC qualification specification that sets out the grading criteria.

Indicative reading
Recommended books, magazines, journals and websites whose content is both suitable and relevant to the unit.

Induction
A short programme of events at the start of a course or work placement designed to give you essential information and introduce you to other people so that you can settle in easily.

Internal verification
The quality checks carried out by nominated tutors at all centres to ensure that all assignments are at the right level and cover appropriate learning outcomes. The checks also ensure that all **assessors** are marking work consistently and to the same standards.

Learning outcomes
The learning and skills you must demonstrate to show that you have learned a unit effectively.

Levels of study
The depth, breadth and complexity of knowledge, understanding and skills required to achieve a qualification determines its level. Level 2 is equivalent to GCSE level (grades A* to C). Level 3 equates to GCE A-level. As you successfully achieve one level, you can progress on to the next. BTEC qualifications are offered at Entry Level, then Levels 1, 2, 3, 4, 5, 6 and 7.

Mandatory units

On a BTEC Level 2 First course, these are the compulsory units that all learners must complete to gain the qualification.

Optional units

Units on your course from which you may be able to make a choice. They help you specialise your skills, knowledge and understanding, and may help progression into work or further education.

Personal, learning and thinking skills (PLTS)

The skills and qualities that improve your ability to work independently and be more effective and confident at work. Opportunities for developing these are a feature of all BTEC First courses. They aren't compulsory to achieve on the course, but are of great use to you.

Plagiarism

Copying someone else's work or work from any other sources (eg the internet) and passing it off as your own. It is strictly forbidden on all courses.

Portfolio

A collection of work compiled by a learner – for an **assessor** – usually as evidence of learning.

Project

A comprehensive piece of work which normally involves original research and planning and investigation, either by an individual or a team. The outcome will vary depending upon the type of project undertaken. For example, it may result in the organisation of a specific event, a demonstration of a skill, a presentation, or a piece of writing.

Tutorial

An individual or small group meeting with your tutor at which you discuss the work you are currently doing and other more general course issues.

Unit content

Details about the topics covered by the unit and the knowledge and skills you need to complete it.

Work placement

Time spent on an employer's premises when you carry out work-based tasks as an employee and also learn about the enterprise to develop your skills and knowledge.

Work-related qualification

A qualification designed to help you to develop the knowledge and understanding you need for a particular area of work.